Helion & Company Limited
Unit 8 Amherst Business Centre
Budbrooke Road
Warwick
CV34 5WE
England
Tel. 01926 499 619
Email: info@helion.co.uk
Website: www.helion.co.uk
Twitter: @helionbooks
https://helionbooks.wordpress.com/

Published by Helion & Company 2026
Text © Stijn Mitzer & Joost Oliemans 2026
Colour profiles: Tom Cooper, Anderson Subtil and
     David Bocquelet
Maps drawn by George Anderson © Helion &
     Company 2026

Cover: A Kumsong-3 AShM is fired from the deck of
     SSES Ib. (KCBC)

Designed and typeset by Mach 3 Solutions
     (www.mach3solutions.co.uk)
Cover design Paul Hewitt, Battlefield Design
     (www.battlefield-design.co.uk)

Every reasonable effort has been made to trace
copyright holders and to obtain their permission
for the use of copyright material. The author and
publisher apologise for any errors or omissions in
this work, and would be grateful if notified of any
corrections that should be incorporated in future
reprints or editions of this book.

ISBN: 978-1-806722-18-1

British Library Cataloguing-in-Publication Data
A catalogue record for this book is available from
the British Library

All rights reserved. No part of this publication
may be reproduced, stored in a retrieval system,
or transmitted, in any form, or by any means,
electronic, mechanical, photocopying, recording or
otherwise, without the express written consent of
Helion & Company Limited.

We always welcome receiving book proposals from
prospective authors.

CONTENTS

Abbreviations and Acronyms   2
Preface   2
Introduction   4

1   Korean People´s Army Navy   5
2   Organisation and Tactics   7
3   Building Up an Indigenous Fleet   12
4   Modern Armaments   23
5   Surface Effect Ships   33
6   Large Ship Construction   39
7   Gunboats and Missile Boats   51
8   Hovercraft   60
9   Submarines   62

Bibliography   77
Endnotes   77
About the Authors   80

ABBREVIATIONS AND ACRONYMS

AIP	air-independent propulsion
AShM	anti-ship missile
ASW	anti-submarine warfare
CDS	coastal defence system
CIA	Central Intelligence Agency
CIWS	close-in weapon system
C4ISR	command, control, communications, computers, intelligence, surveillance and reconnaissance
DMZ	Korean Demilitarized Zone
DoD	Department of Defense
DPRK	Democratic People's Republic of Korea
ECM	electronic countermeasures
EO	electro-optical
FAC	fast attack craft
KCBC	Korean Central Broadcasting Committee
KCNA	Korean Central News Agency
KPA	Korean People's Army
KPAAF	Korean People's Army Air and Anti-Air Force
KPAGF	Korean People's Army Ground Force
KPAN	Korean People's Army Navy
MANPADS	man-portable air-defence system
MoD	Ministry of Defence
MRL	multiple rocket launcher
NATO	North Atlantic Treaty Organization
NLL	Northern Limit Line
NLOS	non-line-of-sight
NMRS	Near-term Mine Reconnaissance System
RCS	radar cross-section
RGB	Reconnaissance General Bureau
ROK	Republic of Korea
ROKN	Republic of Korea Navy
SAM	surface-to-air missile
SES	surface effect ship
SHORAD	short-range air-defence
SLBM	submarine-launched ballistic missile
SLCM	submarine-launched cruise missile
SOF	Special Operations Force
SSB	sub-surface ballistic (ballistic missile submarine)
SSBN	sub-surface ballistic nuclear (nuclear ballistic missile submarine)
SSES	stealth surface effect ship
USV	unmanned surface vessel
UN	United Nations
US	United States
USA	United States of America
USN	United States Navy
VLS	vertical launching system
VSV	very slender vessel
WPK	Workers' Party of Korea

PREFACE

The DPRK. Shrouded in mysticism and secrecy, the nation represents an absolute unicum for the military analyst. No other country in the world manages to attract so much scrutiny to its controversial antics, yet divulge so little of material importance about its inner workings. This might be at the heart of why this country specifically has gripped our attention for so many years, and drawn us to write this series about its largely mysterious armed forces.

Before we introduce the main subject, a couple of clarifications and disclaimers regarding the contents of this book. Since all claims made represent the latest analysis of current military matters in a country that is notoriously secretive, some are bound to turn out to be incorrect as new information comes to light. Wherever a claim is made that cannot be established with absolute certainty, it is clarified through appropriate qualifiers: plausible, likely, and all variations of like sort. Sources are mentioned for those claims that do not bank on our own work, when they are absent it may be assumed that the claim is either an original finding of the authors or held to be common knowledge.

As the subject we have written on mainly concerns the DPRK, it is the North Korean romanisation scheme of Korean that we have attempted to adhere to for most Korean names, which differs from those schemes common in the South. In some cases this might be cause for confusion, further clarification of what exactly is referenced is then usually provided. In similar vein, designations of the Korean People's Army's various branches are matched to their North Korean analogues, abbreviations of which are adopted as follows: Korean People's Army, KPA; Korean People's Army's Ground Force, KPAGF; Korean People's Army Air and Anti-Air Force, KPAAF; Korean People's Army Navy, KPAN; Special Operations Force, SOF; Missile General Bureau, MGB.[1] These branches also serve as the main structure of this book series, and are treated in the order listed above. We'd also like to express our profound gratitude to our dear friend Tarao, whose aid in researching and promoting this project has been indispensable. Furthermore, the variety of talented artists that have contributed to the many wonderful artworks deserve nothing but praise.[2] Any questions on this publication or related matters are more than welcome, and may be directed to onthepathofsongun@outlook.com.

A map of North Korea with the most important locations mentioned in the volume. (Map by George Anderson)

INTRODUCTION

Friday, 9:22PM (GMT+9), 26 March 2010

An explosion rocks the *Cheonan*, a Pohang-class corvette of the South Korean Navy carrying a crew of 104 on a routine coastal patrol near the disputed waters of Baengnyeong Island and the Northern Limit Line (NLL). The sheer force of the blast causes the ship to break in half just minutes later, a hastily scrambled rescue mission failing to save the lives of 46 missing sailors, most of which were trapped aboard the sinking vessel. The *Cheonan*'s active sonar had failed to detect the threat looming in the waters below: a North Korean submarine that had been lurking in the area for the past day. Waiting at a depth of 30 metres for the *Cheonan* to pass it by, it had kept its torpedoes ready to strike at an unsuspecting target. After forcing a torpedo out of one of its launch tubes with a violent burst of expanding gases, the wake-homing device then sought its way to the soft underbelly of the *Cheonan*, breaking its back with the explosive force of its 250kg warhead. As suddenly as the unprovoked attack had commenced its effects would subside again, with the vessel sinking at approximately 9:30PM. The submarine that had caused this tragedy slipped back into the dark waters of the North unnoticed, leaving a nation reeling in grief, anger and confusion in its wake.

In the initial chaos following the sinking few knew where to place blame for this great loss of life. The South's Ministry of Defence (ROK MoD) in its press briefings urged for restraint while an investigation was set up, and some suggested an internal explosion or an old sea mine might have been responsible. But no, the *Cheonan*'s fate was not decided in an unfortunate split second of some unintended detonation. Instead, as much as weeks before, gears started turning that would eventually cause the event that brought two nations to the brink of war, and changed the inter-Korean dynamics for the better part of a decade. Still, little-to-no concrete evidence of the North's culpability in those prior weeks exists, and the first indication that anything out of the ordinary was apace came just over a week before the sinking. Five KPAAF MiG-29 aircraft forward deployed to Kwail air base and another five MiG-23s at Hwangju indicated a highly unusual state of alertness not seen outside of staged exercises or provocations in the DPRK. At the time, the joint United States Forces Korea/Republic of Korea Army Foal Eagle/Key Resolve exercises were coming to a close, which the North Koreans have since their inception condemned as the cover for an invasion of the North – thus potentially providing an explanation for this deviation from the norm. Nevertheless, with the exercises having ended on 18 March, a detachment of two submarines, one Yeono-class and one Sang O-class, accompanied by a support ship, left their home port at the Pipagot naval base on the 23rd. Reportedly, on its mission to the South the smaller Yeono-class subsequently detoured to the west side of Baengyeong Island on the 25th, and there awaited the passing of the *Cheonan*. When the suitable target of opportunity had been found and doomed, the North Korean vessels broke off their mission and reberthed at Pipagot on the 28th.[3]

In the following months, the resulting Republic of Korea (ROK) investigation swiftly came to the conclusion that a North Korean torpedo indeed was overwhelmingly likely to have been the culprit for the sinking. Famously, most of its remains (complete with Korean markings) were actually recovered and matched with the schematics of a North Korean manufactured CHT-02D torpedo. Vehement denials and lengthy rebuttals of the investigation's findings by the Korean Central News Agency (the DPRK's state news) expressed the official North Korean stance on the matter, and tensions between the two nations rose sharply as economic and diplomatic sanctions were imposed by the South. Although the incident was not the first case of open hostilities between the two nations in recent history, it was the final nail in the coffin for the relatively stable relations and closer cooperation brought on by the so-called Sunshine Policy – heralding the start of a decade of confrontations and mutual animosity. That the pain inflicted by the *Cheonan* sinking has anything but subsided today was attested by the angry response of many to the choice of sending Kim Yong Chol as the head of the North Korean delegation to the closing ceremony of the 2018 Winter Olympics in Pyeongchang. As former director of the infamous Reconnaissance General Bureau (RGB), he was accused of having masterminded attacks such as the one on the *Cheonan*, and his continued prominence as a political figure in the North highlights the difficulties that lie in store for a possible reconciliation between the two countries.

Some have claimed the sinking of the *Cheonan* was a mere coincidental strike against a target of opportunity by an overzealous submarine commander, but in truth the incident fits into the larger context of North Korean provocations that have typified its aggressive foreign policies since its founding. These planned provocations often serve as the basis for the rise to power of an important figure within the Workers' Party of Korea (WPK) or KPA, or otherwise are conducted for symbolic reasons, to prove loyalty, or even simply as an act of revenge. As anticipatory measures the DPRK nowadays usually mobilises fighter aircraft, air-defence systems and anti-ship missiles (AShMs) in the general vicinity of where a resulting confrontation might take place. In committing acts that fall short of outright triggering a war, the DPRK has been able to seriously influence its neighbours, and in the least retain its place in the international spotlight given that its economical and political influence are nowadays insufficient to do so. The potentially colossal humanitarian and financial catastrophe brought on by the onset of full-scale hostilities has in the past often been enough to discourage the ROK and USA from retaliating militarily, though only through exercising great restraint. Provocations such as these, whether they occur close to the Korean Demilitarized Zone (DMZ) or even in entirely different nations, are the staple of inter-Korean relations and provide a stark reminder of the fact that a renewed conflict is never far away. Given that the economical and technological situation in the two Koreas are nowadays more in contrast than any two bordering countries in the world, the reason why this threat remains so potent might be obscure to some. However, despite the fact that in the past decades the KPA has suffered much in terms of technological prowess and overall upkeep relative to its Southern neighbour, in considering its current strength its ability to import weapons and technology from abroad (especially before the sanctions regime) is often underestimated, and the capabilities of its indigenous military industry even more so. Some of these acquisitions lean on old relations with like-minded governments, others simply exploit the black market; others still are of surprising sophistication, and suggest some larger geopolitical game is at play, presumably motivated by a Russian and Chinese desire to uphold North Korea's status as a buffer zone between these countries and Western-aligned South Korea. It is the latter category that has allowed the DPRK to reverse-engineer or otherwise copy sensitive weapons systems and technologies such as the S-300 air-defence system, Kh-35 anti-ship missile and an advanced 300mm multiple rocket launcher, not to mention a myriad of developments related to its ballistic missile programme. In more recent years, the pace at which new designs, sometimes with a clear foreign influence, at other times entirely original, have appeared is unmatched even by some major powers. Research, development and particularly the production of these systems (often within short timeframes) by the North Koreans is impressive, potentially indicative of an outside influence that has aided them. Whatever the case, it has not only enabled a revival of the KPA as a fighting force, but also helped keep the DPRK's military exports competitive during an age of ever-tightening sanctions. North Korean arms stemming from the past half-century remain abundant across the globe, and as it produces (or formerly produced) many of the weapons systems Soviet-aligned nations were supplied with, it is a source of affordable maintenance and upgrades. Its efforts at keeping these – now illegal

– exports a secret constitute some of the toughest challenges to the United Nations (UN) in dealing with the nation, each year spawning extensive investigations and expansions of sanctions. Were it not for the unrelenting pressure exerted on other UN members to adhere to the embargoes in place, North Korea would likely be a major arms exporter, generating much revenue for a state known for its economic hardship, as well as allowing it to regain some of the influence decades of isolation have bereft it of. Of course, the days where the DPRK could boast of substantial economic gains and widespread political clout have long gone. In an age then where its adversaries enjoy a massive technological and economical advantage, and its traditional allies for the first time show hesitation in their resolve, the North's navy faces an unclear future. Will it wither in the shadow of North Korea's blooming nuclear arsenal, or will stubborn adherence to the Songun (military first) doctrine allow it to soldier on?

1

KOREAN PEOPLE´S ARMY NAVY

The Korean People's Army Navy, historically the most severely underreported branch of North Korea's armed forces, nevertheless has received some of the most ambitious designs that have come from the DPRK's military industry. However, the lack of public information on the KPAN's capabilities for a long time lent it a reputation of solely operating outdated ships, as well as lacking the funding to maintain what inventory it has. Not only does this stereotype lack nuance, the often-echoed presumption that the KPAN is incapable of introducing new technologies is simply incorrect. A largely dormant but surprisingly innovative shipbuilding industry has silently kept the KPAN in play while more substantial projects evaded attention, positioning it for a radical expansion of its roles in the near future. The transition to larger shipbuilding and 'blue water' aspirations in the mid 2020s can be partly explained through this perspective, although it remains one of the more astonishing upheavals in North Korea's varied military history.

As with the other branches of the KPA, the KPAN started using indigenous designs quite early and on an ambitious scale. It began improving and producing various copies of foreign designs, torpedo boats and miniature submarines in the 1950s and 1960s, moving on to building full-sized frigates and experimental designs in the 1970s and 1980s, and in the 1990s and twenty-first century began designing advanced stealth craft, ballistic missile submarines, guided-missile destroyers and a whole array of other modern naval vessels.

A North Korean naval force was first established under the title of Maritime Security Force on 5 June 1946, which is nowadays celebrated as Navy Day in the DPRK. Historically, the DPRK's interests in having a strong navy came to be during the Korean War. Although neither the North nor the South had a very large navy during this conflict, the United States Navy (USN) was very active around the Korean Peninsula, providing both coastal fire-support and logistical support to forces battling the communist regime's infantry on the ground. The KPAN consisted of several 1930s Soviet G-5 motor torpedo boats backed up by a myriad of miscellaneous vessels armed with several guns of different calibres at this time. The few naval engagements between North Korean torpedo boats

and the USN resulted in a clear defeat for the North as a rule, and almost all damage done to USN ships was inflicted either by shore batteries or sea mines. All the same, the DPRK still claims to have sunk several major vessels including the heavy cruiser USS *Baltimore* and a British destroyer using four Soviet G-5 motor torpedo boats during the Battle of Jumunjin, which took place in 1950 and actually saw three USN and Royal Navy vessels destroy three North Korean torpedo boats. Interestingly, USS *Baltimore* was not actually in commission during the battle, nor was it ever deployed to Korea during the Korean War. While the DPRK highly inflates its naval successes during the Korean War, it did attain some success by the use of coastal artillery and through the laying of minefields, which damaged dozens of ships and sank five US Navy vessels, including four minesweepers.[1] North Korea adheres to completely different statistics itself, and maintains that 25 enemy warships were sunk or destroyed in the first three months of the Korean War alone, mounting to 564 by the time hostilities concluded.[2]

The mainstay of the KPAN during the Korean War consisted of a hodgepodge of civilian ships converted to military use. Ships like these were used for patrol tasks and resupply missions along the Korean Peninsula. (KCBC)

After the war, naval skirmishes continued at regular intervals, sometimes escalating to full-sized battles claiming the lives of many. One of the first true naval victories for North Korea that is frequently cited as such by propaganda broadcasts was the sinking of the Patrol Craft *Dangpo*, on 19 January 1967 by coastal batteries on the east coast. Further successes included the sinking of the *I-2* near Yeonpyeong Island on the west coast in June 1970 after the ship was overwhelmed by a group of North Korean patrol craft. A similar incident occurred a few years later, when Patrol Boat *No. 863* of the Korean Coast Guard was sunk on the east coast on 28 June 1974 after a firefight with North Korean patrol craft. It is notable that all three ships were guarding South Korean fishing vessels at their time of sinking. The protection of fishing fleets became a necessity after the KPAN started harassing South Korean fishing vessels operating alongside the demarcation line throughout the 1950s and 1980s, but also extending into the 1990s. This harassment campaign was aimed at the capture or else sinking of South Korean vessels, resulting in the abduction, and at times killing, of thousands of fishermen, of whom hundreds never returned to the South.

Another notable early incident was the capture of the USN intelligence gathering ship USS *Pueblo* on 23 January 1968. This incident resulted in 82 sailors being captured and a single sailor being shot dead, considerably increasing tensions between the DPRK and the USA. There were some claims that North Korea would bring the ship into service, but it was instead towed from the east coast to the west coast in 1999 to be displayed in Pyongyang, and was subsequently moved to the recently constructed Fatherland Liberation War Museum in late 2012. Here it joined an American 'spy torpedo', a device claimed to be an unmanned underwater surveillance vehicle captured in 2004 near the city of Hamhung on the east coast.[3] The vehicle appears to have been part of the US Navy's Near-term Mine Reconnaissance System (NMRS), a stop-gap project to provide an interim mine reconnaissance capability while a successor was under development.[4] With only two prototypes ever built, the NMRS programme was terminated in May 2005; the loss of one of the prototypes might well have played a role in this decision. Smaller scale incidents continued to occur after the *Pueblo* incident, yet it would take another 30-odd years before a series of naval clashes started escalating sharply.

Centred around the maritime borders of North and South Korea's western coast, the onset of this period of clashes was heralded by what is now known as the First Battle of Yeonpyeong. Brought on by North Korean naval vessels deliberately crossing the disputed NLL on several occasions, initial ramming manoeuvres between 9 and 12 June 1999 prompted increasing numbers of naval vessels from both sides to be deployed to the area.[5] On 15 June, the situation escalated after the ramming of a North Korean torpedo boat was responded to with small arms fire and shots from its 25mm dual cannon. The ensuing confrontation left the seven North Korean vessels outnumbered by 16 larger and better armed Republic of Korea Navy (ROKN) craft, and resulted in the sinking of one torpedo boat and upwards of 17 deaths on the KPAN's side. By contrast, the South Koreans sustained only slight damage and seven injured crew members. Not surprisingly, in the KCNA narrative published days after the event it was the South Korean craft that initiated fire, as part of a preplanned provocation, and which suffered numerous casualties as well as at least 10 burned or severely damaged warships.[6]

In an apparent act of revenge, two North Korean naval craft once more crossed the NLL on 29 June 2002 and engaged two ROKN Chamsuri-class patrol boats that responded to the incursion. The opening shot fired from one of the KPAN craft's 85mm cannon at 450 metres range immediately struck the *PKM-357*, severely damaging it. The *PKM-357* later sank while under tow, and total casualties on the Southern side numbered six killed and another 18 wounded. The offending North Korean naval vessel was last seen burning fiercely, though it is believed to have made its way to port under tow, and according to South Korea 13 North Koreans lost their lives, in addition to 25 wounded.[7] This Second Battle of Yeonpyeong was followed by another skirmish of similar nature in 2009, now known as the Battle of Daechong. A North Korean patrol boat that had strayed south of the NLL responded to warning shots by opening fire, ultimately resulting in an exchange of fire which slightly damaged a South Korean patrol craft and left the Northern side with an unknown number of casualties. These events set the stage for the incidents of 2010, against a backdrop of the KPAN's transformation from a massive yet technologically limited navy to a force incorporating modern technologies on a large diversity of craft.

The South Korean Patrol Craft *Dangpo* sinks after having been hit by North Korean coastal artillery in 1967. (KCBC)

A South Korean Chamsuri-class patrol boat rams a North Korean gunboat after the latter crossed the disputed NLL in the First Battle of Yeonpyeong 1999. A Chamsuri-class patrol boat identical to this one was later sunk by the North during the Second Battle of Yeonpyeong in 2002. (ROK MoD)

2

ORGANISATION AND TACTICS

Numerically speaking the KPAN is one of the larger navies in the world, with over 470 surface vessels, 250 amphibious craft, 70 submarines and an estimated 60,000 personnel. Nonetheless, as the North Korean military remains primarily a land-based force the KPAN is the smallest of the three major branches, and operations are complicated by the fact that South Korea separates the North's two coastlines. This has effectively meant that the KPAN is divided into an East Sea and a West Sea Fleet, the two of which are nowadays almost completely cut off from each other. Headquartered in Rakwon, the KPAN's East Sea Fleet is the largest of the two fleets, with over two dozen harbours under its command. Major ports include Namae, Songjon, Rakwon, Mayang Do, Chaho and Puam Dong, with a major new port under construction at Munchon. The West Sea Fleet is headquartered in Nampho, and its largest ports include Sagot, Koampo, Cho Do, Pipagot, Nampho, Kibong Dong and Tasa Ri. Major shipbuilding construction facilities are located in Nampho, Rajin, Wonsan and Sinpho. In addition to these, there

are several smaller construction facilities present in Pyongyang, Chongjin and Yongchong, each serving their own particular role. The shipbuilding industry has not yet overcome its difficulties in swiftly outputting new vessels, a major problem that continues to thwart the modernisation efforts of the KPAN today. The production of vessels can progress at an incredibly slow pace, and as a result, even ships from the same class can differ enormously. While the 2010s briefly saw some improvement in the speed of construction of ship hulls, the outfitting of ships with weapons systems, radars and other equipment can often take up to several years as well, and the period of accelerated shipbuilding was followed again by one marked mainly by inactivity. Sea trials usually take place at the location of construction, sometimes adding another several years before a vessel is finally assigned to its designated unit, assuming no significant issues arose in the process. When resource allocation and political will align, projects can also materialise at miraculous speeds however, as two destroyers built and outfitted in little more

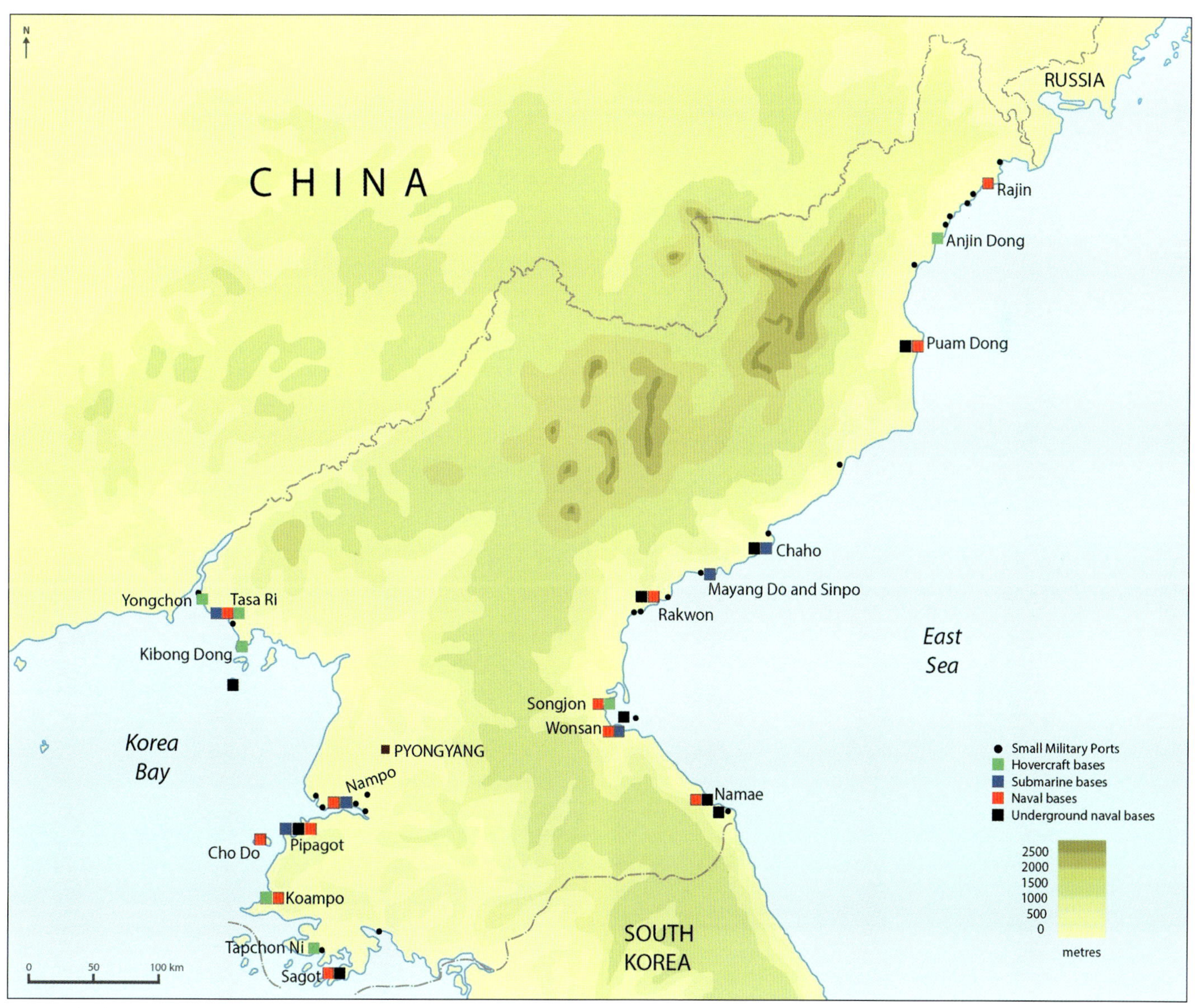

A map of military ports and naval bases in North Korea. (Map by George Anderson)

than a year attest. This performance remains the exception rather than the norm, and is likely the result of careful planning as well as foreign assistance.

When a vessel is finally commissioned, many KPAN ships spend the vast majority of their career in harbour or stored on land, a reflection of their size and role as much as the scarcity of exercises. Even the few larger seaworthy ships that actually have a chance of directly competing with ROKN or USN vessels rarely venture out to sea for long periods, with patrol and fishery protection usually carried out by smaller vessels and gunboats. While most ships are well maintained, to which they owe their longevity, a relatively large number of KPAN vessels are lost due to accidents. This is partly due to the age of North Korea's fleet, but also due to its immense size, unsafe practices and the poor quality of rescue vessels. In a rare case of transparency about its safety record, North Korea admitted to the costly loss of an SO.1-class submarine chaser on 13 October 2013 on its eastern coast, resulting in the deaths of its entire crew of some 30 sailors.[1] As with other branches of the KPA, a lack of fuel prevents adequate training and exercises at sea, and especially exercises of combined forces from multiple bases appear scarce. To compensate for a lack of sailing hours, simulators for a variety of training scenarios exist for most ship types, including submarines. While they provide a different experience than would be obtained

actually out at sea, these simulators can at least partly compensate for the lack of actual exercises. In the instances when real life exercises are depicted in propaganda footage, scenarios played out tend to be a poor reflection of reality, including for instance the firing of torpedoes at islands.

Due to the geographical location of the Korean Peninsula, the Korean People's Army Navy has committed many of its resources in the East Sea, where the threat of US ships and in particular carrier groups is the highest. Headquartered in Pyongyang, the Korean People's Army Navy is composed of two fleet commands, 13 naval squadrons and two maritime sniper brigades. In addition, each coast can call upon coastal defence missile batteries for the defence of harbours and cities. Furthermore, the East Sea Fleet has a dedicated naval aviation squadron for anti-submarine warfare. Although many of the designations are similar to those of the army and air force, there are some notable differences between the two. The KPAN refers to its naval forces as squadrons, 13 of which are known to exist. Squadrons include all ships, which are further divided into Flotillas, which each operate one type of ship. As with the KPAGF and KPAAF, bases also carry a Unit designation, with Combined Unit 587 referring to the West Sea Fleet and Combined Unit 597 to the East Sea Fleet. Both shipyards and units can have honorific titles. Examples of this are the October 3 Dockyard, which was built as the country's first base for warship repair in July 1947 at the instruction of President Kim Il Sung; and KPA Naval Unit 167 honoured with the title of O Jung Hup-led 7th Regiment and Guards 2nd Surface Ship Flotilla.

Until recently, North Korea defied common international standards by not naming its ships, and most designations associated with their indigenous industry originate from US DoD naming schemes, usually referring to cities where the ships were first sighted. Instead, vessels are referred to by simply using a number and sometimes type designation, such as Patrol Ship *No. 661* (for an Amnok-class corvette). The only exceptions to these rules were in its exports, where vessels are given names that refer to their basic properties such as length and type, an example of which is the MS 29 – a 29-metre long midget submarine. Since the 2010s, ships and boats have come to receive both class designations and individual names, of which the Choe Hyon-class destroyer whose lead ship is also named *Choe Hyon* is a notable example. In line with this trend,

Kim Jong Un pays his respects at a memorial to the sailors of submarine chaser 233, which sank in late 2013. (KCBC)

A Type 033 submarine fires a torpedo at an island. Although the idea behind this move might have been that the island represents a US aircraft carrier, such exercise scenarios still mainly aim to please the leadership watching these exercises. (KCBC)

Most bases have an infrastructure capable of performing maintenance work and limited modernisation on a range of KPAN vessels. In this case, three Chaho-class fire-support vessels armed with eight 200mm rockets have been brought onto land at Pipagot naval base on the DPRK's west coast. (Authors' archive)

Among North Korea's most modern naval craft is the Choe Hyon-class destroyer *Choe Hyon*. The vessel was one of the first surface combatants in the KPAN to receive an actual name instead of a type designation and hull number. The hull number 51 is likely a subtle jab at the USS *Arleigh Burke* (DDG-51), the lead ship of its class and a symbol of US naval dominance. (KCBC)

future warships are to be named after prominent revolutionaries.[2] In addition to the vessels operated by the KPAN, several other agencies also operate ships, including the Reconnaissance General Bureau, and the Coastal Security Bureau. The Coastal Security Bureau is in effect a militarised Coast Guard and is primarily responsible for guarding North Korea's sea borders, with a secondary role of harbour security and fishery protection. In practice however, the primary task of the Coastal Security Bureau is to prevent illegal departure out of the DPRK by sea. The vessels it operates mainly comprise patrol craft, some 150 to 200 in number, and is thus limited in its firepower. Most vessels are unarmed, and those that are usually employ light weaponry only. In times of war, the assets of the Coastal Security Bureau likely fall under the jurisdiction of the KPAN. Similarly, commercial vessels ranging from fishing boats to larger cargo ships may well be claimed for use by the KPAN during war, although due to the nature of its force composition the roles they could fulfil are limited.

While the Korean People's Army Navy possesses one of the largest fleets in the world, its surface fleet is configured primarily for operations along the coast, traditionally featuring little in terms of large surface combatants. The two Amnok- and two Tuman-class corvettes, along with two Najin-class frigates until recently constituted the most capable ships of their respective sizes and are distributed evenly on each coast. In the mid 2020s, they were joined by two Choe Hyon-class guided-missile destroyers, signalling a transition towards more conventional shipbuilding and a more assertive naval posture which seeks to commission additional destroyers and even a cruiser in the near future. They join a mixed fleet with remnants

of a multitude of different innovation drives, with the latest arguably dating back to the early 2000s and 2010s. Five Nongo-class surface effect ships (SES) spearheaded this renewed modernisation push in the 1990s and early 2000s, being also the first to be armed with North Korea's 76mm OTO Melara copy and the new Kumsong-3 AShM. The Haesam-class stealth surface effect ships (SSES) was developed from the technology used on the preceding Nongo-class, but went further to incorporate increasing stealth elements in its design. Other major vessels, dating back to the previous century, comprise two 1930s-era Fugas-class minesweepers and four indigenous Sariwon-class corvettes, all completely antiquated by today's standards and best classified as little more than gunboats. Although deemed to be of a dated concept in the West, North Korea continues to operate significant numbers of such surface combatants, including the SO.1, Type 062, Type 037, Taechong I and Taechong II, which represent a mixture of Soviet, Chinese and North Korean designs. Although they are generally over 60 metres long and equipped with many large-calibre guns, they would be of limited use in modern conflict aside from presenting a target for enemy cruise missiles, and policing of coastal waters and use in provocations during peacetime. The KPAN has introduced several types of newer gun and patrol boats into service in recent years, making effective use of several types of newly developed rotary guns, whose high rate of fire and radar guidance mean these vessels retain some combat relevance in today's missile-dominated naval warfare.

Despite a change in doctrine signalled by larger vessel construction, the KPAN is still mostly equipped for coastal warfare, and the vast majority of its inventory consists of vessels of smaller than 40 metres in length. Roughly 350 fast attack craft (FAC) armed with torpedoes, small gunboats, minesweepers, landing support ships and patrol boats buff the KPAN's numbers and form the bulk of its inventory. These are mostly of North Korean design built during the 1970s and 1980s and are based on earlier Soviet and Chinese vessels dating from the 1950s and 1960s. Often smaller craft such as these are not based at larger ports but instead rely on smaller storage facilities on land, sometimes equipped with their own underground shelters. In recent years, new classes of torpedo boats have been developed which incorporate semi-submersible characteristics and new types of torpedoes. However, of these only an ambitious offshoot in the shape of the Very Slender Vessel (VSV) class have thus far entered service in the DPRK, with more conventional torpedo boats mainly aimed at export. In addition to these lighter craft the KPAN relies on another 50 or so guided-missile boats mainly of the Soviet Komar

Vessels like these Yongdo-class patrol craft belong to the Coastal Security Bureau, and mainly operate along the Yalu river separating the DPRK with China and along the sea border with South Korea on either coast. (KCBC)

A 533mm torpedo being pushed towards a torpedo boat. Although North Korea already received its first AShM-equipped ships in the mid 1960s, the venerable torpedo still plays a central role even today. (KCBC)

and Osa I type and the North Korean copies of these respective ships. Increasing introduction of armament such as the Kumsong-3 AShM and non-line-of-sight (NLOS) missile has meant that smaller classes of new warships are now likely to become increasingly equipped with modern guided munitions. They usually feature only modest radar suites however, relying on efficient C4ISR (Command, control, communications, computers, intelligence, surveillance and reconnaissance) and synergy with larger combatants for their efficacy.

The trend of smaller vessels optimised for coastal warfare is continued with North Korea's submarine fleet, most indigenous offshoots of which have been in the midget submarine size class. Nonetheless, its investments in this branch have been anything if not ambitious, and its submarine forces are some of the largest in the world in terms of sheer numbers, comprising over 25 large attack submarines of the antiquated 1950s Soviet Whiskey and 1960s Chinese Type 033-class submarines, as well as a myriad of small classes built indigenously since the late 1970s. The larger Soviet and Chinese legacy attack submarines are used in a conventional manner, and despite the fact that they are no match for any sufficiently modern opponent their size means that they are the sole examples capable of operations on the high seas. In more recent times, the emphasis has lain on the design and production of guided-missile submarines, including the initiation of a nuclear-powered submarine project.

Closer to shore, a still growing fleet of infiltration and hunter-killer submarines sits optimised to operate close to coastal areas and at times rely on support vessels to increase their range. These small, relatively slow but silent submarines are optimally used during peacetime, as evidenced, for instance, by the sinking of the *Cheonan* in 2010 and the infiltration missions of the 1990s. During wartime their poor mobility would hinder effective operations, but their stealthiness and number means they could still wreak havoc amongst enemy combatants and support vessels venturing too close to the coastlines. Although operating a large fleet of submarines, North Korea has no modern specialised anti-submarine warfare ships, though many ships have a rudimentary anti-submarine warfare (ASW) capability. The only dedicated ASW assets are the Air Force's Ka-28s and Mi-14s, which do not appear to be currently deployed in this capacity however. The sole exception to these underwhelming ASW capabilities is the new Choe Hyon-class multirole destroyer, which features sonar, anti-submarine missiles and torpedoes, and possibly even ASW-configured vertical take-off and landing (VTOL) drones.

The KPAN's offensive operations are supported by scores of landing ships of various sizes and up to 200 hovercraft. All but the larger landing ships are limited to transporting infantry, with amphibious fire-support provided by vehicles such as the 323 armoured personnel carrier and Sinhung light tank carried only by the largest examples in service. As the wartime insertion of large numbers of forces through amphibious means is likely to attract massive attention from opposing sea and air assets, the use of many smaller craft instead of large vessels in modern times is a necessary strategy to enhance their chance of survival. In a similar vein, North Korea operates the largest hovercraft forces in the world, yet consisting mainly of vessels below 22 metres in length. Built during the 1980s and 1990s, this force struggles to maintain its relevance in an era of advanced maritime surveillance and smart munitions. Nonetheless, when used to their maximum potential up to 8,000 infantry, mainly belonging to the KPAN's maritime sniper brigades, could be inserted into a coastal area on each haul. In modern times, some modest research into newer hovercraft designs has resumed, albeit for now solely aimed at the export market.

On the defensive side, an important part of its naval strategy is dictated by the laying of extensive minefields, stemming from the successes gained in such manner during the Korean War but also such conflicts as the Iran-Iraq War. Although the KPAN operates no dedicated minelayers, many of its vessels have the capacity for minelaying, including its modest inventory of minesweepers and even commercial vessels such as cargo and fishing ships. Using the cover of peacetime or currents, minefields could be extended to enemy coastal waters and the high seas, and submarines can be used for a more deliberate insertion of sea mines into key straits. Although details on modern North Korean mines are sketchy, they likely have relatively advanced technology given how important they are to the KPAN's strategies. Nonetheless, even its mix of older types in use since the Korean War could present a major threat, primarily to amphibious landing ships and other ships operating in coastal areas, due to the large numbers concerned.

Although officially under the command of the KPA's Ground Forces, coastal artillery also plays an important role in the naval defence of the DPRK. Both during the Korean War and since, such gun systems inflicted significant casualties amongst US Navy ships and the occasional South Korean vessel, which has likely led to their popularity in the DPRK today. Most coastal artillery comprises calibres ranging from 100mm to 152mm, with the Soviet 130mm M-46 and SM-4-1 (which was designed specifically for this role) being the most powerful and longest ranged. Some smaller calibre guns, light 107mm multiple rocket launchers (MRLs) and even anti-tank weaponry, including guns and anti-tank guided missiles, are also used for coastal defence, mainly for countering amphibious invasions. Such defences are typically housed in hardened shelters dug out of coastal rock formations, while others use simpler entrenched positions. Massive numbers of pre-prepared positions along the DPRK's long coastlines exist for use against a possible invasion force, often consisting of little more than simple revetments. KPA units, such as the rear corps, would quickly be deployed to such areas when an invasion looms. The KPAN has also operated various types of coastal defence missile systems (CDS) since the 1960s, many of which are nowadays highly mobile and, as such, difficult to target. Such systems have been the subject of much technological investment in previous decades, and today the DPRK's most advanced examples present perhaps the single largest threat to opposing naval forces of all weaponry in service with the KPAN. Still, they remain mostly reliant on the detection of enemy vessels by vulnerable coastal defence radars or large naval assets, or more cumbersome electro-optical (EO) devices and reconnaissance aircraft. When such systems are dismantled or suppressed, the efficacy of any CDS is greatly diminished no matter their potential range.

In the initial stages of a conflict however, the KPAN is likely to be fully engaged on the offensive, using its submarines and FACs to engage ROKN ships near South Korean coasts and enable amphibious operations. To this end, its hovercraft forces and landing support ships would commence landing manoeuvres while support craft, such as those vessels equipped with MRLs, would attempt to suppress coastal defences. To prevent the successful operation of the ROKN and US Navy it would also immediately attempt to mine approaches to ports and important sea lanes, prolonging the initial phase of the war in which the KPAN may yet hold the advantage for as long as possible. Once the tide has turned, it would then shift its priorities towards the defence of North Korean harbours and vulnerable coastal areas, having little hope of effectively engaging the overwhelming naval presence of its enemies at this stage. Crucial to this strategy of initial high intensity offensives is a high state of readiness, which is reflected in the locations of its primary naval bases. The bulk of these can be found in the southern half of the country, below the Taedong River on the west coast and the Chaho submarine base in the east. Nevertheless, actual preparedness levels within the KPAN appear to be quite low, and should a war break out that is not strictly on its terms many of its combatants could be caught without munitions or while undergoing overhauls. For instance, its older guided-missile boats still use variants of the P-15

Termit which require careful fuelling with dangerous chemicals prior to their use, and newer AShMs are typically not seen mounted during peacetime.

Should these ships get to sea, they would find themselves at odds against at least one greatly superior navy in terms of equipment. A lack of both air power and defensive means against enemy aircraft will likely ensure that the operational life of the average KPAN ship during wartime will be exceptionally short. The larger the vessel the more likely it is to attract enemy fire, explaining why the DPRK has mainly focussed its efforts on smaller and cheaper vessels as opposed to capital ships as its acquisition strategy. The myriad of underground shelters employed at various bases may lengthen the average lifespan of its ships somewhat, but with modern precision-guided munitions and proper reconnaissance any ship caught unprepared will soon be destroyed. Although it is often depicted in North Korean propaganda facing off against the USA's aircraft carriers, this brings up the important consideration of whether the KPAN would even be afloat by the time US carrier groups arrived in the region. These factors perhaps elucidate why in the 2020s a notable doctrinal shift saw North Korean naval production reoriented towards smaller numbers of large missile-carrying vessels. While they theoretically stand a better chance against the aforementioned threats, they simultaneously present a clear priority target for opposing forces. Without the ability to attain parity in naval production, asymmetric warfare may well constitute the KPAN's best bet, for better or worse.

Above left: Kim Jong Un inspects a copy of the 130mm M-46 towed field gun, which is designated the Type-68 in the DPRK and often used in the coastal defence role. (KCBC)

Above right: Kim Jong Il walks along the quay with a Komar-class missile boat in the back. Note the empty missile canisters: missiles would only be loaded just prior to combat. (KCBC)

Right: A North Korean crew works a 130mm SM-4-1 coastal defence gun during an exercise. Unlike the M-46, the SM-4-1 was designed for this role. (KCBC)

3

BUILDING UP AN INDIGENOUS FLEET

In keeping with its Juche ideology and mirroring developments within the Korean People's Army Ground Forces, a large part of the KPAN's inventory is 'Made in the DPRK'. The KPAN started indigenous shipbuilding efforts in the 1960s and soon stopped importing military vessels, meaning that all craft introduced since the 1970s were produced, and often designed, indigenously. However, prior to these developments the DPRK still exclusively relied on the Soviet Union and China for its inventory, and the roots of many of even its most modern designs can still be traced back to these countries. As with other branches of the KPA, the KPAN had to be rebuilt after losing much of its already dated inventory during the Korean War. As the bulk of the KPAN's offensive fleet had consisted of motor torpedo boats, it was only logical that the expansion program launched after the signing of the Armistice placed a heavy emphasis on such fast and agile craft. This marked the beginning of the acquisition of large numbers of Soviet and Chinese torpedo boats, mainly of the Project 123K (P-4) and Project 183 (P-6) series. The P-4 and later P-6-class were delivered to the KPAN in limited numbers, most of which are still in active service today. These craft would prove to do very well in the DPRK, and would later serve as the basis of many indigenously-produced variants. The P-4-class was equipped with two 450mm torpedo tubes and a dual 14.5mm mount, whereas boats of the P-6-class are armed with two 533mm torpedo tubes and two dual 2M3 25mm weapon stations: a considerable improvement over its predecessor. These boats were later supplemented by a large number of Chinese Type 025-class hydrofoil torpedo boats, which can easily be discerned from the similar P-4-class by their forward-mounted hydrofoils, allowing for increased speed.

The bridge of a North Korean torpedo boat, which protects its operators against neither gunfire nor rainfall. (KCBC)

The first larger ships that reached the then still fledgling KPAN were two Fugas-class minesweepers (commonly, yet incorrectly, known as the Tral-class), donated by the Soviet Union shortly after the Second World War. Interestingly, it appears these ships were held back in the Soviet Union awaiting a more stable situation allowing for their delivery, which took place after the signing of the Armistice Agreement in 1953. Originally designed in the early 1930s, these ships were constructed throughout the following decade, seeing heavy action during the Second World War. Their intended role was to operate in the confined waters of the Caspian and Baltic Sea as opposed to the open ocean, limiting them mainly to coastal

A North Korean P-6-class torpedo boat passes alongside a Soviet warship off the Korean coast. (KCBC)

operations around the Korean Peninsula. Their armament was very unremarkable by the time they entered service with the KPAN, with a 100mm turretless gun on the bow comprising their main weaponry, the open mount of which would not even protect its operators from simple rainfall, let alone shrapnel. One ship was upgraded during the 1980s to serve as a gunboat, featuring a turreted 85mm gun on the bow, a platform for four ZPU-4s and two dual 37mm cannon stations at the aft. This updated armament meant its minesweeping equipment was removed in accordance with its new role as a gunboat. The original Fugas-class also formed the basis for the design of the Sariwon-class corvettes, which by the virtue of its armament could also better be classified as a gunboat. This class, one of the first of the North's larger ship designs, signified the start of North Korea's ambitions of becoming self-sufficient in the design and construction of warships. Produced throughout the late 1960s, the four Sariwon-class ships came with various improvements over the original Fugas, most notable of which is a redesigned bow and a more generic-shaped bridge replacing the inconveniently small one seen on the Fugas-class. The armament was virtually unchanged from the original Fugas, with a platform for four dual-barrelled 14.5mm ZPU-4s around the funnel and an armoured casemate around the large-calibre gun being the only exceptions. The entire class was modified variously throughout the 1970s and 1980s, and ships differ mainly from one another by their armament and bridge layout.

The sole Fugas-class minesweeper still in unmodified state, showing its 37mm cannons. (KCBC)

A Sariwon-class corvette in a standoff against a ROKN vessel. (ROK MoD)

A modified Fugas-class gunboat in 1993, clearly showing its turreted 85mm gun, four 14.5mm ZPU-4s and dual 37mm cannons. (US DoD)

Although the Sariwon-class corvettes remain some of the larger ships produced by the DPRK to date, the production of this class also emphasised that it was still heavily reliant on foreign designs for the basis for its indigenous shipbuilding programmes, a fact further attested by the copying of the Soviet SO.1 submarine chaser in the same period. The DPRK had taken delivery of its first SO.1 submarine chasers in the early 1960s after which around a dozen improved examples were subsequently built indigenously according to its own shipbuilding standards. Ironically, this meant that the ships lost their original ASW task and were outfitted as gunboats instead. While the original design only included two 25mm 2M3 dual cannons for self-defence, the indigenously built variant saw the mounting of one casemated 100mm on the bow, two 37mm cannon stations at the aft and one 25mm 2M3 dual cannon on a raised structure midships. The Chodo-class was constructed at roughly the same time to a similar design template but featured an open-topped 85mm turret on the bow and further variations in armament. The introduction of the up-gunned SO.1s and the indigenously built variants of other ships marked the start of a build-up of a large fleet of gunboats for coastal operations, replacing the hodgepodge of improvised coastal combatants dating from the 1930s and 1940s previously used in this role. Although nowadays the gunboat concept has been relegated to the annals of history by most nations, the gunboat remains one of the most active types of ship in service with the KPAN, and the North is still actively producing new types today. While their outdated but large-calibre weaponry has meant the gunboat has taken part in most naval skirmishes with the South, their combat efficiency in a conventional war is likely to be extremely limited in the AShM-rich environment of today.

Apart from striving to become self-sufficient in the construction of various types of naval vessels, the 1960s also marked the start of another highly ambitious project with the aim of protecting large parts of the KPAN fleet by carving out huge naval bases in mountains along the east and west coasts. These underground naval bases are so well protected by metres of rock, that the thick walls remain impenetrable by most conventional bombs and artillery shells today. However, modern bunker-busting munitions are more than likely to penetrate the thick walls, making these underground bases outdated to a certain degree. Due to the immense size of these underground naval bases, construction would go on for decades, and has resulted in a dozen underground naval bases of various sizes being available to the KPAN on each coast today. Although some differ little from other bases housing contingents of small fast attack craft, others likely stretch on beyond the coast for hundreds of metres, with the Chaho underground bases even storing Type 033-class submarines which measure 76.6 metres in length.

The 1960s also advanced the KPAN into the missile era when the DPRK started acquiring its first anti-ship missiles from the Soviet Union and China. The Soviets delivered small numbers of Komar-class missile boats in the mid 1960s to reinforce its large fleet of torpedo boats, which were later supplemented by the more modern Osa I-class missile boats, carrying four P-15 Termit AShMs instead of the Komar's two, acquired from the Soviet Union.[1] It was during the same period that the Soviet Union delivered the earlier S-2 Sopka coastal defence missile system, some missiles of which reportedly came in knock-down kits to be assembled in the DPRK.[2] However, presumably due to a reluctance to provide more missiles, North Korea turned to China for the delivery of more equipment. This resulted in China delivering the HY-1 missile system and aiding with the setting up of production facilities for these systems, which are designated the Kumsong in the DPRK.[3] These production facilities would later be converted to produce the improved HY-2 missile, which could only be used in the coastal defence role due to its large body. As the ROKN only began to deploy AShMs during the early 1980s, with a single project initiated in the late 1970s ending in failure, the KPAN clearly held the advantage in this area for almost two decades.

Another notable relic of this period that is still in use is the Soviet Project 206 'Shershen-class' torpedo boat, of which at least four were

In the unlikely wartime event of a North Korean gunboat coming within (effective) firing range of ROKN vessels, the seemingly well-armed gunboats would be quickly outmanoeuvred by the more agile ROKN craft with rapid-firing cannons in hydraulic rotating turrets. While generally equipped with larger calibre but slower firing cannons, most turrets on KPAN ships are still rotated by hand. Pictured: an up-gunned SO.1-class. (ROKN)

The 100mm cannon seen here on three SO.1-class craft are now also seen on several variants of modern-built ships. (KCBC)

An underground naval base on the west coast. Although its sizeable facilities run through the entire hill, this base is actually one of the less significant ones at the KPAN's disposal. (Google Earth – Image © 2019 Digital Globe)

A rare image of North Korean S-2 Sopka coastal defence missile systems during the 40th anniversary of the Korean People's Revolutionary Army parade in April 1972. (KCBC)

delivered as early as 1968.[4] These boats represent the most modern imported class of torpedo boats in North Korean service. Carrying twice as many torpedoes as most other North Korean torpedo boats as well as being equipped with two twin 30mm AK-230s directed by an MR-104 'Drum Tilt' radar, these craft are still actively used in the DPRK. However, no attempt at copying the design has ever been made, most likely because the ship's capabilities did not warrant the importation or production of the expensive systems involved.

Instead, the DPRK began constructing large numbers of fast attack craft and patrol boats based on the designs and experience gained with operating the fast attack craft it had received from the Soviet Union and China. This considerable programme entailed the construction of various types of vessels often based on the same hull, thereby increasing conformity and ease of production. These craft, in addition to various types of vessels produced in smaller numbers, still constitute the mainstay of the KPAN, in effect forming

A Shershen-class along with its missile-carrying brothers of the Project 205 Osa I-class (or North Korean Soju-class) at Rakwon naval base. (KCBC)

the largest FAC fleet in the world, albeit highly outdated. Their large diversity has complicated naming schemes used by the US DoD to identify individual types, and many subvariants exist that do not appear to have any designation. Some also appear to have entered service with the Coastal Security Bureau, and others were exported to friendly nations during the Cold War where they are no longer in active service.

The most prevalent amongst these designs is the Sinhung-class, more than 100 and possibly up to 140 of which were produced until the late 1980s, despite the fact that it mainly constituted pre-1960s technology. Three variants were made: a regular FAC, a FAC which incorporated hydrofoil technology (possibly utilising up to 10 imported British-made navalised Proteus engines), and a patrol boat.[5] In the latter capacity they are sometimes referred to as the Kusong-class, which closely resemble the even smaller Yongdo- and Kimjin-class which have the same gun armament on smaller hulls. Twelve of these patrol boats were delivered to Nicaragua in the early 1980s, in addition to two Kimjin-class.[6, 7, 8] Benin, Guyana, Madagascar and Mozambique are also reported to have received patrol boats of unknown make in the same time frame.[9] In the FAC configurations the Sinhung-class was armed with two 533mm torpedoes and two 14.5mm mounts, while the patrol boat version only carried the two 14.5mm mounts. Another slightly larger fast attack craft is known as the Sinnam-class and is equipped with the same armament as the Sinhung – yet another one is armed with two single 37mm cannons and a 2M3 25mm weapon station and is referred to as the Sinpho-class. These boats supplemented the externally similar Chinese Shantou-class gunboat, which also entered service with the KPAN. The FACs with torpedoes still have a limited role in modern conflict, simply due to the sheer numbers available. It will be a lot harder to find a suitable role for the gunboats and patrol craft in wartime conditions however, which are mainly relegated to peacetime patrol missions and provocations.

More significant would be the development and construction of a series of landing craft and fire-support vessels based on modified P-6 hulls, known by the US DoD as the Nampho-class, Chongjin-class, and Chaho-class. The Nampho-class craft, only equipped with two 14.5mm weapon mounts, are designed to transport and disembark forces while the Chongjin-class and Chaho-class provide fire-support with their heavy weaponry. The Chongjin-class was armed with an 85mm turreted cannon and two 25mm 2M3 when it was first produced, providing it with a surprisingly effective means to destroy smaller enemy combatants and conduct limited coastal battery missions. The Chaho-class on the other hand is equipped with an MRL installation which could be used to suppress enemy defensive positions along wide areas so forces could then be inserted by craft such as the Nampho-class (which no longer appears to be in use). Both a variant sporting eight of the BMD-20's 200mm rockets and one using the 40-tubed BM-21's 122mm rockets are in use, the latter presumably produced after the 122mm system came to be widely introduced into the KPA. Both rockets have a similar range of up to 20 kilometres, but the 122mm system is clearly superior with its far larger payload consisting of forty 20 kilogram warheads as opposed to eight 30 kilogram warheads for the 200mm system. Both variants utilise an automated reload system to provide a second salvo at short notice. Roughly 100 Nampho-class, 50 Chongjin-class and 50 Chaho-class have been constructed since 1971, although most, if not all, Nampho-class boats have been converted to patrol boats and many craft have also been retired.[10] Further offshoots of the P-4/6 design are the Yukto I- and Yukto II- (also known as the Pipa A) class minesweepers, the latter of which replaced the former and was

A cutaway model of a modernised P-6-class torpedo boat at the Pyongyang Sci-Tech Complex. A product of a bygone age: yet ready to enter battle at any time serving the KPAN. (KCBC)

A Sinhung-class hydrofoil. These torpedo boats reach extremely high speeds, yet despite extensive experimentation with the concept they were produced in relatively limited numbers. (KCBC)

Once armed with 2x 14.5mm twin mounts, most Kusong-class patrol boats now carry rotary guns of the same calibre. (US DoD)

A Chinese Shantou-class gunboat in KPAN service. (KCBC)

Sailors aboard a Chongjin-class gunboat in a celebratory moment. Also note the two 14.5mm rotary machine guns on the aft. (KCBC)

Four Chaho-class fast attack craft equipped with eight 200mm rockets taken from the BMD-20 MRL. (KCBC)

A look at the Chaho-class's unique loading capability, inspired by the similar capabilities of its second generation 122mm MRL systems. A second salvo of 40x122mm rockets is loaded into the launcher as a gunner manning a 14.5mm rotary machine gun provides overwatch. (KCBC)

A Type 062 leaves port alongside a host of other gunboats during an exercise. (KCBC)

slightly smaller, forgoing the aft weapon station. Limited numbers of these craft still see service, presumably more in the minelaying role than as minesweepers however.

To further strengthen its growing fleet of gunboats, North Korea acquired 12 Type 062-class gunboats (NATO designation Shanghai) from China in the mid to late 1960s, supplementing the up-gunned SO.1s that were being built at that time. At just under 39 metres, these ships were slightly smaller than the 42-metre long SO.1s, a limitation which is reflected in the Type 062s' armament. One dual 37mm cannon station on the bow and another dual 37mm cannon station aft provide the ship's main armament, two 25mm 2M3 dual cannons are carried midships and a recoilless rifle on the bow provides heavier firepower for close range skirmishes. The Type 062 would later serve as the basis for another indigenously-produced gunboat, which can be further divided into at least two subvariants, each equipped with a different weapon suite and bridge layout. A further Chinese product to have entered service with the KPAN is the Type 037 submarine chaser (NATO designation Hainan), at least six of which are believed to have entered service on the west coast. The Type 037 is a Chinese take on the Soviet SO.1 submarine chaser, albeit substantially larger at 58 metres, large numbers of which were exported to several other nations. Although the ships

Despite the introduction of 14.5mm rotary machine guns to a host of KPAN vessels, the venerable 25mm 2M3 remains the primary anti-aircraft gun on most older types of craft – with some even carrying both types. Seen in the back is a 37mm dual cannon station. (KCBC)

Kim Jong Un poses with the crew of a Type 037. Like all types delivered from China, these ships are only stationed on the west coast. (KCBC)

in Chinese service would receive several upgrades during their career, the examples operated by the KPAN remain quite similar to the standard of the SO.1. Featuring the same four RBU-1200 anti-submarine rocket launchers, improvements mainly came through the addition of two dual 57mm weapon stations on the bow and aft.

Having received both the Soviet SO.1 and its Chinese successor the Type 037, the DPRK subsequently used this proven design as the basis for an up-gunned derivative with a length of some 60 metres. These ships became known as the Taechong-class, a relatively successful conventional design which continues to serve in the KPAN today. The Taechongs were a progressive development of the Chinese Hainan-class, optimised for operations along the Korean coast. Much of the original Chinese design was retained, with the addition of heavier weaponry, an altered bridge and a different sensor outfit comprising the main differences between the two. At least 12 ships are believed to have been completed, making the type one of the most numerous large gunboats currently in service. The Taechongs can be divided into two separate production batches, commonly known as the Taechong I and Taechong II respectively, with several subvariants of each. Laid down throughout the 1970s and 1980s, the first batch consisted of at least seven vessels. The dual 57mm gun station on the bow seen on the Hainans was replaced by a single turretless or, more commonly, casemated 100mm gun, while some ships were outfitted with a turreted 85mm gun instead. The platform in front of the bridge was widened to allow the placement of a second 25mm 2M3 dual cannon or two dual 14.5mm mounts. The number of RBU-1200 anti-submarine rocket launchers was reduced from four to two, although some ships of the class carry no launchers at all. At least three different variations of these ships exist, each with further differences in armament and superstructure.

A Taechong I-class is outmanoeuvred by several ROKN Chamsuri-class patrol boats during the First Battle of Yeonpyeong 1999. The KPAN's gunboats are highly vulnerable to flanking due to the slow turn rate of their large-calibre guns. (ROK MoD)

The Taechong-class's more advanced second production batch is commonly referred to as the Taechong II-class. Although having largely the same dimensions and appearance, the Taechong IIs were slightly longer and sometimes featured a heavily redesigned bridge and weaponry, awkwardly placing the new subclass halfway between a gunboat and a corvette. Up to five ships were produced from the early 1980s onwards, likely to counter the growing fleet of ROKN destroyers, the number of which meanwhile surpassed the quantity of combat-capable ocean-going ships operated by the KPAN, to which only two Najin-class ships could really be counted. While the ships of the first batch are still regularly seen during exercises and in videos, the Taechong IIs have only rarely been sighted since their introduction into service. The limited footage that does exist

A Taechong I-class, featuring 14.mm rotary cannon stations (but also the original 25mm 2M3 stations near its aft) and a 100mm gun on the bow. (KCBC)

The anti-aircraft firepower of some of the Taechong II-class vessels was greatly improved compared to the earlier Taechong I-class through the addition of two AK-230s guided by a MR-104 Drum Tilt radar. (KCBC)

provided valuable clues about their career however, as at least some ships are now equipped with two AK-230s located at the fore and aft of the ship. The associated MR-104 Drum Tilt radar was placed midships.

Although the design and construction of the Taechong-class marked the end of the mass production of gunboats, the KPAN has introduced several types of gunboats since, albeit in smaller numbers. Perhaps the most significant of these is also the most elusive, so far only rarely appearing in state media. This 56-metre long one-off is equipped with one turreted 85mm cannon on the bow and a dual 57mm gun station aft, and named the Mayang-class by the US DoD. A further eight weapon stations of a smaller calibre, including two 25mm 2M3 dual cannons in front of the bridge and six 14.5mm weapon stations beef up the ship's anti-aircraft defences. Still other early designs exist, and another rarely seen gunboat is designated as the K 48-class by the US DoD. Armed with a large-calibre cannon, supposedly 76mm (not to be confused with the modern-day OTO Melara copy of the same calibre), on the front deck and up to three 37mm M-1939 anti-aircraft guns on the aft, this craft likely constitutes the remnants of one of the earliest gunboat manufacture programmes in the DPRK, initiated in the early 1960s or even 1950s.

While the KPAN had built up a considerable force of gunboats and torpedo-armed fast attack craft during the 1980s, the Komar- and Osa I-class were also indigenously-produced during the 1980s

with minor modifications as the Sohung- and Soju-class, respectively, to provide an indigenous guided-missile capability. These have been manufactured in numbers surpassing those originally imported, and still form the mainstay of the AShM-equipped fast attack craft fleet. While the Sohung-class appears to be a direct copy of the Komar, the Soju-class is remarkable in that it was lengthened about four metres from the bridge onwards. No changes in armament are apparent however, and while the Chinese copy of the Osa I was often equipped with the 25mm 2M3 dual cannon, the North Korean Soju-class retained the two twin 30mm AK-230s. In recent years, Osa I- and Soju-class craft have increasingly been stripped of their MR-104 Drum Tilt radars however, with manual aiming stations taking their place. This was presumably done because the AK-230 has only limited anti-air utility in modern combat anyway, and the radars were required for newly built vessels. A Soju-class derivative gunboat armed with a 100mm turret on the front bow, two 14.5mm mounts located next to the bridge and two 25mm 2M3s and two double-barrelled 37mm mounts on the aft entered service on the east coast in limited numbers. Interestingly, the DPRK apparently also intended to produce a class that combined the 85mm gun of the Chongjin with the multiple rocket launcher of the Chaho, designated the Chongju-class, but of the nine ships produced between 1974 and 1975, only one Chongju-class had this configuration before being stripped again in 1976. The other ships were converted to fast attack craft, three of which had P-15 AShMs, and the others were converted to patrol boats or were retired.[11]

Having produced roughly 100 Nampho-class landing craft and some smaller boats, such as the Hungnam-class used in the same role, North Korea then set out to produce larger landing craft that could also transport and facilitate the landing of armoured fighting vehicles. The two types concerned are designated the Hanchon- and

A rare image of a Sohung-class missile boat. (KCBC)

Its modern-looking bridge might lead one to mistake this craft for a modern warship, whereas in reality it is the rarely spotted Mayang-class gunboat. (KCBC)

The aft of a Soju-class gunboat. Note the depth charges, 37mm dual cannons, 25mm cannons and the 14.5mm ZPU-2 mounts mounted next to the bridge. (KCBC)

Hantae-class, measuring in at 36 and 47 metres respectively. While the Hanchon-class was little more than a large barge with a hinged ramp, not even utilising an internal hull for sheltered storage of its passengers, the Hantae-class featured four 25mm 2M3 weapons stations and a unique bow visor allowing for swift disembarking relative to its size. Nonetheless, it still holds three armoured vehicles at the very most, and North Korea's entire fleet of large landing craft on both coasts combined would be able to haul fewer than a hundred armoured vehicles at any given time, a very underwhelming number indeed. Unsurprisingly, their influence on the outcome of a future war would therefore be very limited.

The first indigenous design of true importance came in the form of the DPRK's first frigates, named the Najin-class by the US DoD. In commission since the early 1970s, these two ships were the flagships of their respective coasts and also the largest indigenous naval product of the DPRK for over half a century, at 103 metres length. The original design, of which two were produced with hull numbers 531 (east coast) and 631 (west coast, later renumbered 591) was armed with a triple 533mm torpedo launcher on a rotary platform in the ship's midsection as well as two 100mm guns near the bow and aft, two 57mm ZIF-31 dual cannons directly behind these, two 25mm 2M3 dual cannons next to the bridge and four 14.5mm ZPU-4 quadruple anti-aircraft guns on a platform next to the aft funnel. Like many other KPAN ship classes, she bears the necessary equipment for minelaying and using depth charges. By the time of their introduction in 1973 this weaponry could hardly be expected to compete with the US Navy's designs. The fact that all of this weaponry had to be aimed, loaded and fired manually and is only capable of reaching some degree of accuracy while the ship is stationary made things even worse, and effectively meant the Najin-class was obsolete in its role the moment it was commissioned. This was the main reason why the craft were modernised during the 1980s, bringing them up to roughly 1960s standard. The triple torpedo launcher and ZPU-4s were removed and the midsection was overhauled to make room for two AShM launchers for variants of the P-15, fitted to fire extremely closely alongside the bridge, making them very dangerous to use and potentially harmful to the ship itself. The class's air-defence capabilities were improved by the addition of two twin 30mm AK-230s directed by an MR-104 Drum Tilt fire-control radar, and four more 25mm 2M3 dual

A Hantae-class landing craft offloads a Sinhung amphibious tank during beach landing exercises. (KCBC)

Kim Jong Il inspects one of the larger landing craft available to the KPAN. (KCBC)

A small landing craft armed with 2x2 14.5mm mounts. The efficacy of such dilapidated barges is highly doubtful. (Uwe Brodrecht)

One of the KPAN's two Najin-class frigates pictured in 1993. (United States Navy)

Kim Jong Il spectates a Najin-class frigate standing on the helicopter deck of the Soho-class. (KCBC)

As ambitious as the design of the Soho-class frigate was for its time, it appears that a series of design flaws resulting in a subpar level of seaworthiness prevented the ship from becoming a success. Although – in contrast with the Najin-class – designed from the onset with AShM operations in mind, the resources wasted on the Soho-class could likely have provided the KPAN with another two Najin frigates, showing that North Korea's incentive to incorporate unconventional and unproven technology into its designs has not always worked out in its favour. Of note is the excessive length of the Soho's flight deck, which would be mirrored in the design of the Tuman-class helicopter corvettes decades later. (Artwork by Anderson Subtil)

cannons, requiring the lifeboats to be placed further to the aft. One could rightfully argue that the Najin-class ultimately presented little more than a heftily equipped gunboat even after its overhaul, yet the fact that it heralded an era of ever more ambitious indigenous ship design is undeniable.

On this note, another highly remarkable project was launched in the late 1970s, and consisted of the building of an experimental twin-hulled helicopter-carrying frigate, named the Soho-class by the US DoD. It measured about 74 metres in length, of which about 30 metres was helicopter landing deck, and was equipped with four AShM launchers for Styx-type descendants, one 100mm gun, two 57mm dual cannons, two twin 30mm AK-230s, two 25mm 2M3 dual cannons and six RBU-1200 anti-submarine rocket launchers. It also carried an indigenously-produced MR-104 Drum Tilt radar for direction of its 30mms, and another radar possibly of the MR-123 'Bass Tilt' type. Being the sole ship in the class, its hull was laid down in 1980 in the north-eastern port of Rajin, receiving the hull number 823 upon completion in 1982.[12] Subsequently, sea trails are thought to have laid bare some serious flaws in its design, leading to it laying mostly moored in Rajin harbour for up to three years after.[13] Complex and radical in its design as it was, the Soho enjoyed a very rocky career even after being moved to Singyo Ri where it would serve until the late 2000s. Presumably due to its very low level of seaworthiness it spent most of its time lying in port until it was finally moved to Rajin and scrapped in 2009, less than 30 years after its inception. Given the fact that many ships dating to as far back as the direct post-war time period are still in active service, this is quite remarkable. All available video footage and imagery of the helicopter deck either show it empty or occupied by a Mi-4/Z-5, and it is likely that in the rare cases that the ship was at sea no helicopter was present. Even though it was certainly a testimony to the ingenuity of North Korean naval engineers, which would not be quelled by these poor results in later years, the ship was essentially a massive waste of resources save for the experience gained.

A 57mm ZIF-31 dual cannon mount. Though they are impressively large, they sport a very low firing rate and accuracy, and are manually loaded and aimed. (KCBC)

A Mi-4/Z-5 helicopter sits on the deck of the Soho-class. It is likely the design was too unstable to actually sport a helicopter on its deck while out at sea. (KCBC)

Kim Il Sung inspects a model of the Soho-class, with a model of the Najin-class visible to the left. (KCBC)

4

MODERN ARMAMENTS

Despite having imported and later constructed large numbers of vessels of different types, enabling the KPAN to build up a clear superiority over the ROKN until the mid 1980s, most North Korean designs had one thing in common: they tended to be outdated by the time they entered service. It achieved its superiority over the ROKN more due to a lack of a serious build-up by the South and a sheer numerical advantage than anything else. With the start of the construction of modern ROKN naval vessels during the 1980s and the deployment of South Korea's first operational AShMs, in the form of the US Harpoon missile, early in the same decade, the KPAN rapidly began to lose the edge it had previously achieved. While ties with the Soviet Union were once again warming during the mid to late 1980s, much of the budget at this time went to acquiring weaponry for the other branches. As a result, the KPAN did not benefit from this short improvement in relations, forcing it to continue to rely on the technology it had previously acquired, or indigenous advancements thereof. The KPAN thus entered the 1990s in crisis, with the technological superiority it had once enjoyed now lost, its traditional supplier, the Soviet Union, dissolved and with the DPRK itself in economic crisis. The future of the KPAN looked grim.

However, it is precisely this environment in which the DPRK's weapons industry managed to flourish: when the odds were stacked against it and ingenuity was required. In the economic disarray of the 1980s and 1990s, the DPRK turned to the few allies it had left for the acquisition of modern technology and weaponry for studying and reverse engineering while continuing work on improving already existing technology, most notably the Styx AShM.[1] Surprisingly, this approach paid off tremendously for the KPAN, allowing the DPRK to access technology it could only have dreamed of years earlier through backchannels rather than the costly purchase of large numbers of weapons directly. At the same time, this period can be seen as one of the strangest in the development of North Korean weapon technology, as the direct result of this approach was the acquisition of several types of notable Western weapon systems. One example of such a system was the French Exocet AShM, several of which were likely transferred from Libya sometime in the 1990s.[2] Although the variant received, the AM39, was air-launched and no direct copy has ever been made, the technologies the North Koreans could access through it provided a wealth of knowledge which it would later apply to its own AShM programmes. Similarly, Iran is believed to have provided the DPRK with several C-802 AShMs it had imported from China in 1999 with the aim of jointly developing an indigenous variant of the missile.[3] Although there is no indication that this actually occurred, C-802 technology may well have found its way into modern North Korean AShMs designs.

Perhaps the most surprising new weapons system that the KPAN premiered in this period was an indigenous copy of the Italian 76mm OTO Melara 76/62 Compact naval artillery system. This rapid-fire automated cannon is in active service with dozens of navies across the globe, mostly in the Western sphere of influence, and was also acquired sometime during the 1990s from Libya. Capable of extremely rapid fire of some 85 rounds per minute, and accurate over large distances against both air and ground targets in part due to its unique revolving magazine, the 76mm OTO Melara represented a significant improvement over any gun system previously available to the KPAN. Past large-calibre cannons as a rule were manually loaded and aimed and therefore cumbersome to use, enjoying no assistance from stabilisation systems or fire-control radars. While some have speculated about a link between the Iranian copy of the 76mm OTO Melara, the Fajr-27, and the North Korean-produced variant, it should be noted that the latter was developed almost a decade before the former and that the Iranian cannon is based on a different OTO Melara 76/62 variant. Reverse engineering and production of the 76mm OTO Melara is no small feat, and it is certain that copious resources must have been invested in this project so that the KPAN's naval vessels of today can employ it. The large size of its below-decks magazine and its fire-control radar also necessitated a new direction of design for many of the warships that would receive it, heralding the adaptation of a novel design philosophy on the whole. Interestingly, the regular fire-control radars associated with this system were not copied, and instead a new one was designed, albeit not yet deployed on every ship carrying the 76mm OTO Melara. Telling of the difficulties the DPRK must have faced in its production, the KPAN's OTO Melara utilises a crudely welded turret casing as opposed to the smooth or stealthily angled examples usually seen abroad. A variant with an angular turret reminiscent of the one on the Otobreda 76/62 Super Rapid was displayed at the Self-Defence-2021 exhibition in October 2021, with the inaugural KPAN vessel outfitted with it being one of the Tuman-class corvettes. Given that the cannon in question was observed firing at a rate of about 95 rounds per minute, its likely internal improvements to the original design were applied as well. Expanding on the angular turret design is a newly developed compact and lightweight mount that seems to have been designed after the 76/62 Sovraponte, and that is being deployed on a new generation of smaller naval ships entering service. Considering that the original copy of the 76mm OTO Melara has only been scarcely introduced on new KPAN naval craft in general, it appears indigenous manufacture of these systems is now progressing steadily.

Another product by OTO Melara copied in recent years is the 127mm OTO 127/64 LW, which constitutes the main gun armament for large craft starting with the Choe Hyon-class destroyers. While it introduces yet another new calibre to an already highly complicated arsenal of shell types, the 127mm gun (also known as the VULCANO system) is a formidable upgrade over previously available systems. While the faithfulness of the copy cannot be ascertained, the original boasts the use of guided rounds with range in excess of 100 kilometres, a firing rate of approximately 32 rounds per minute, and a highly automated modular feeding magazine with 56 rounds ready to fire. With both the 127mm and the 76mm Sovraponte constituting some of the most modern naval armaments on offer by OTO Melara (now Leonardo S.p.A.), there is no obvious source for either technology beyond a security leak.

While the various OTO-inspired products are limited to newly built ships due to its size restrictions, another development of the 1990s would transform smaller calibre weaponry on nearly every class, including those already in service. Building on the huge success of the ZPU-4 and the 14.5x114mm calibre in the DPRK, it gave birth to a rotary machine gun in this calibre that would provide even greater firepower in a smaller and much more ergonomic shape. The result, a small manually-aimed 14.5mm weapon station, is easily placed on warships of any size and provides heavy firepower at close range. It replaces many light calibre weapons stations on DPRK craft of all sizes, although it should be mentioned that outdated weaponry such as the 25mm 2M3 is sometimes retained, presumably due to the much greater destructive power of the 25x218mmSR round. Additionally, the 14.5mm rotary machine gun is still of little use against jet aircraft and serves mainly to tear up smaller opposing craft or helicopters. To provide the true close-in

weapon system (CIWS) which KPAN naval vessels of the 1980s and earlier sorely lacked, a programme was initiated at the start of the 1990s for the development of a ground- and ship-based air-defence weapon. Despite the fact that the AK-230's enclosed turret was used as a basis for the design, the resulting 30mm six-barrelled rotary gun system itself appears to be largely identical to the Soviet AK-630. The far-reaching similarity between the North Korean variant and its inspiration likely indicates a technology transfer between the Soviet Union and the DPRK sometime during the late 1980s or early 1990s, although no naval craft sporting the original AK-630 CIWS has ever been exported to North Korea. With a blistering fire rate of some 5,000 powerful 30mm rounds per minute, radar guidance and an effective range of four kilometres it is the first system with a chance of providing protection against cruise missiles, while being light enough to be installed on most ships which would otherwise be capable of carrying the AK-230. On North Korean naval combatants the system is often slaved to the MR-104 Drum Tilt, instead of the more modern MR-123 Bass Tilt typically associated with the AK-630, although the radar used for the OTO Melara copy (including a new variant) is also compatible with it.

A much improved CIWS was first showcased in 2025, and may be set to replace the AK-630-derived design on all future naval vessels. Exchanging the classic Soviet turret for a mount modelled after that of the Dutch Goalkeeper CIWS, it retains the sextuple 30mm barrels while adding an integrated fire-control radar and EO device. While the design is similar to both the aforementioned Dutch type and the Chinese Type 730, various design decisions are distinct from either and it is likely to draw inspiration from these types only. While no tests have yet been publicised, the integrated control systems should constitute a substantial improvement in performance. Likewise, the new mount is thought to enhance its rotation speed and recoil mitigation while obviating the need for a below-deck magazine.

No dedicated surface-to-air missiles (SAMs) have historically ever been mounted on KPAN ships, and their survivability against aircraft therefore remains low. Nonetheless, complementing the AK-630-derived CIWS mounted on new ship designs is a small SAM station which allows an operator to fire up to six MANPADS-derived missiles at incoming aircraft. While this is obviously unlikely to provide much compensation for the lack of true SAM systems on naval craft which are typical on modern vessels abroad, the small size of this station means it can be mounted on virtually any craft and thus expand the threat that the North's ubiquitous man-portable air-defence systems (MANPADS) pose on land to the sea. Most of

A starboard view of a SES II, showing the indigenous copy of the 76mm OTO Melara on the foredeck. (KCBC)

The front deck of the destroyer Choe Hyon, showcasing its 127mm OTO 127/64 LW copy during weapons tests. (KCBC)

The first model of the 14.5mm rotary machine gun station, which is equipped with a comparatively small magazine. Note the armoured panels hanging in front and over the gunner's seat. While this model has meanwhile been superseded by a more modern design with increased capacity, it continues to make up nearly all of the 14.5mm rotary machine guns deployed on KPAN ships. (KCBC)

The second variant of the 14.5mm rotary machine gun station was first seen deployed on Myanmar naval craft. In North Korean service they have only been sighted on the new 77 metre corvettes currently entering service. The larger type of magazine, sleek design and lack of armoured panels are clearly visible here. (Tatmadaw – Myawaddy TV)

North Korea's copy of the 30mm AK-630 CIWS aboard a Myanmar Navy craft. Note the enclosed turret of the AK-230 used for the system. (Tatmadaw – Myawaddy TV)

A burst of rockets is seen firing from one of the two 40-barrelled decoy launchers mounted on either side of the Choe Hyon-class destroyer. The hatches housing the two 14.5mm rotary machine guns on either side are visibly open. Farther towards the rear a 14.5mm KPV can just barely be made out, part of its close-in defence suite. (KCBC)

North Korea's newest CIWS. Note the integrated EO device and fire-control radar, and the lack of the shell ejection mechanism found on the Type 730. (KCBC)

the small SAM stations in service with the Myanmar Navy have been automated, eliminating the need for manual guidance. It is currently unknown if this is a North Korean or Myanmarese invention. On craft that are too small to carry the MANPADS station a similar solution has been found in an even smaller mount for just two MANPADS. When active measures fail, the KPAN can still resort to obscuring their ships from view through the use of 82mm chaff/smoke launchers. These six-tubed systems are nowadays found on virtually every KPAN naval craft, having been developed during the 1980s for the laying of smoke screens or fooling radar-guided weaponry. On the newest ships, these have been replaced by turreted launchers sporting 40 tubes each.

A North Korean small SAM station and its operator aboard a Myanmar Navy craft, clearly showing the six slots where MANPADS can be fitted. (Tatmadaw – Myawaddy TV)

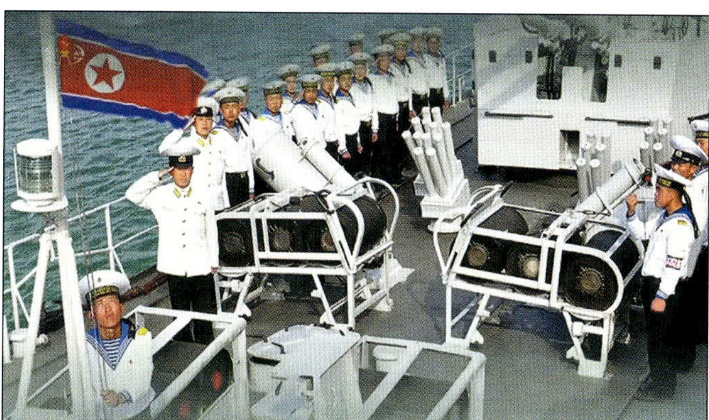

A Type 037 showing its crew on the rear deck. Note the prominent depth charges, the 57mm Type 66 cannon and the four 82mm chaff launchers; the latter are a North Korean addition. (KCBC)

Two North Korean 30mm CIWS aboard a Myanmar Navy craft. Note their fire-control radar in the middle (thought to be a second generation North Korean design), and the boxy SAM station. Leftmost, a 76mm OTO Melara. (Tatmadaw – Myawaddy TV)

These rather modest defences are now being superseded by much more robust missile capabilities on the DPRK's newest naval craft. This is partly enabled by the gradual availability of a new generation of domestic short, medium and long-range air-defence systems, as well as investments in vertical launching system (VLS) technology. The systems involved are a navalised version of the Pyoljji-1 long-range SAM and what is believed to be a navalised variant of the Pyoljji-3, although the Pyoljji-2 would be similarly suitable. While the Pyoljji-3 and especially the Pyoljji-1 constitute a major leap in both ship protection and sea-based power projection, neither has proven anti-missile capabilities. Even if such capabilities are eventually demonstrated, it remains a daunting task to ensure survivability against modern (i.e. sea-skimming, coordinating and/or supersonic) AShMs without a layered defence network distributed among multiple naval vessels. The long and short-range missile systems of indigenous design are complemented by a product of one of the more egregious breaches of international sanctions since Russia's reconciliation with North Korea. While Korean name plates and small differences in construction details betray indigenous manufacture, the overall design of this combined gun-missile system is nigh identical to the Russian Pantsir-ME heavy CIWS. Sporting two six-barrelled 30×165mm rotary cannons and eight missile tubes slaved to an integrated 1RS-3 reflective phased array radar and EO/IR (electro-optical/infrared)

device, it can independently engage aerial threats from up to 40 kilometres distance. Up to three different missiles with different characteristics (including a miniaturised anti-drone variant) are available in Russian usage, but thus far only a copy of the 57E6M-E has been displayed. This missile has only recently begun to be introduced with Russian air defences, and is variously accredited with a range of either 30 or 40 kilometres and a remarkable speed of around Mach 5. Neither the gun system nor the missile has yet been demonstrated, but given that it likely concerns licensed production development may not be exceedingly challenging. Currently the deployment of these systems is limited to the new Choe Hyon-class destroyers, where the Pantsir-ME copies however lack the under-deck magazines that allow for automated reloading of their missiles.

On the offensive side, new armament to replace ineffective torpedoes and P-15-type AShMs found its origin in the 1990s. Derived from the very similar Russian Kh-35 AShM, these North Korean missiles, named the Kumsong-3, were developed somewhere around the turn of the century, yet only gained international attention after they were featured in a series of publicised exercises since mid 2014. Tests are thought to have been conducted as early as 2003 however, and it is this missile that seems to have started the new naming scheme abroad, receiving the designation KN-01 for the air-launched variant (US DoD designation Stormpetrel). Later,

A Pyoljji-1 missile is launched from the aft VLS of the destroyer *Choe Hyon* during weapons tests in April 2025, before its refit. (KCBC)

North Korea's newest CIWS, a flagrant copy of the Pantsir-ME, during the launch of the *Choe Hyon* in April 2025. Note that there are no hatches in the deck that could facilitate reloading of the missile tubes. (KCBC)

the designation KN-05 was also used to refer to the CDS variant. Although it is in many aspects very much akin to its Russian predecessor, it is unknown to what degree the North Korean military industry was capable of replicating the delicate radar and engine components it incorporates, and several external differences point to changes in capability, albeit not necessarily for the worse. For one, the entire missile has been lengthened to 5.4 metres (or 4.5 metres without booster), in order to extend its range beyond the 130 kilometres of the Kh-35 and possibly to increase its payload, which was formerly best suited for destroying vessels up to 5,000 tonnes. The rocket booster, which allows it to be fired in surface-to-surface capacity, does not appear to have been changed in size or shape, but a different method of attachment to the rest of the missile and the presence of an exhaust nozzle indicate a significant change in its workings. However, since the booster has only a limited task in firing the missile, this has likely not been detrimental to its performance. Of course, some of the most important components cannot be examined using imagery of its external features only, and some of the Kh-35's particularly useful capabilities might not have been properly replicated.[4] For instance, the active radar seeker's homing range appears to be slightly shorter at 15 kilometres compared to the ARGS-35E's 20 kilometres. Other dissimilarities between the North Korean and Russian missiles can be found in the racks on which the missiles are mounted, and the canisters from which they are fired, presumably made necessary due to the increase in length of the missile, and special requirements for the launchers which will become apparent later on.

Even though it was first deployed in the early 2000s, further development of this system has continued throughout the 2000s and 2010s, and during the parade for the 105th anniversary of Kim Il Sung's birthday in 2017 a new CDS (US DoD designation KN-19) was displayed which utilised advanced Kumsong-3 technology. A publicised test of this system in June of the same year showed extensive modifications to the original specifications of the missile, expanding upon its original capabilities. For one, it displayed a range of at least 250 kilometres, using global navigation satellite system (GNSS) guidance to trace preprogrammed waypoints so as to give it the option of using advanced attack strategies on difficult targets. The original radar seeker was expanded upon with IR guidance, meaning it can switch off its radar on its final approach to increase its survivability against ECM (Electronic countermeasures) and systems that detect radar. Such capabilities bring it on a par with other modern CDS being introduced by nations across the globe to this day, and allow it to execute attacks on well-defended targets by, for instance, timing the arrival of multiple missiles from various directions. Four missile tubes are used on each launcher, which utilises the Chonma-216/Songun-915's T-72 inspired chassis – a 323 APC-based launcher with two tubes was also used, but presumably only as a prototype. The 75th anniversary of the Workers' Party of Korea parade in 2020 introduced a modernised variant of this launcher that uses an armoured cabin overhanging to the front of the vehicle, thus saving up space on the main body of the chassis for eight canisters instead of four. North Korea designates this system and missile as the Padasuri-6 ('fish eagle'), suggesting that other North Korean CDSs of the past carried the designation Padasuri as well. The missile features several changes from earlier versions of the system, notably a new rocket booster lacking fins and a colour scheme of white and grey, as opposed to the previous green finish. Other modifications to the missile could have been introduced, but their exact nature is currently undisclosed. However, it is possible that the Padasuri-6 or one of the earlier Kh-35 derived missiles introduced an improved engine; while the Kh-35 originally used the Ukrainian R-95-300 turbofan, Kim Jong Un in 2023 inspected what appears to be a TRDD-50A engine, which has largely replaced the R-95-300 in newly built Russian cruise missiles. If such Russian-delivered technologies indeed underpin the new North Korean missiles, it could explain part of the performance enhancements over the original Kh-35. Since the tubes of the new CDS were not modified compared to the earlier naval variants, it would appear that the upgraded missiles can also be retrofitted to any naval craft previously capable of using the earlier Kumsong-3s.

Although the Kumsong-3 is similar to the Russian Kh-35, several differences are apparent, including a larger overall length, different booster attachment and an exhaust nozzle. (KCBC)

The Kumsong-3-based CDS based on the Chonma-216/Songun-915's T-72 inspired chassis. While these launchers were originally adorned with a blue camouflage pattern, they nowadays feature a more practical green livery. (KCBC)

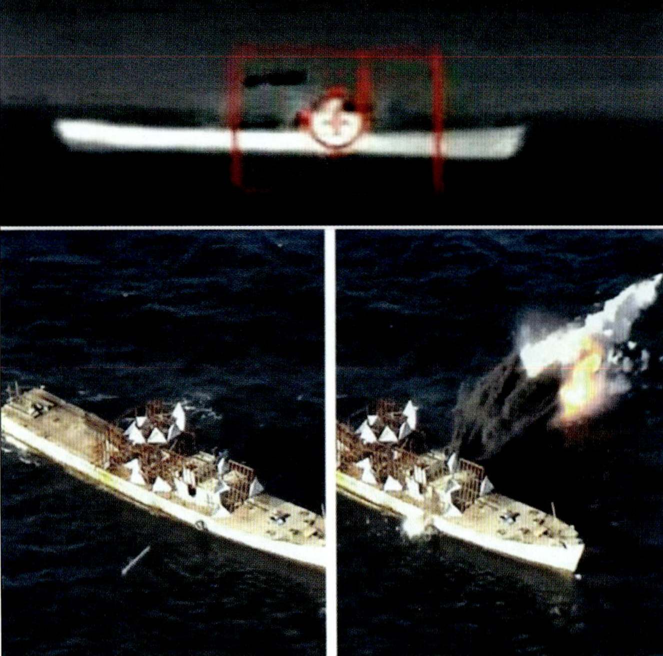

The view from a Kumsong-3s IR-seeker as relayed during a test, and its effect upon striking a decommissioned SO.1 type gunboat. Note the radar reflectors that serve to enhance the ship's visibility to radar. (KCBC)

To supplement the Kumsong-3 against lighter targets, another missile has gradually begun entering service with the KPAN. Making its debut as a ground-based weapon during the parade for the 70th anniversary of the foundation of the DPRK in September 2018, the system appears to be a copy or close derivative of the Chinese CM-501GA land-attack missile. That missile has a range of 40 kilometres, which would be long enough to present a substantial threat to naval targets as well. Accordingly, a coastal defence variant was developed and first showcased during the 90th anniversary of the Korean People's Revolutionary Army in April 2022. Based on a lightly armoured car, it features an integrated surface search radar for independent target acquisition and carries eight launch tubes. A navalised turret with four launch tubes was also first unveiled in October 2021, further underlining the perceived utility of this system in the anti-ship role. Due to its very compact size, virtually any North Korean naval craft is eligible to be outfitted with such a turret, thus potentially vastly extending their range, firepower and flexibility. Of course, the compact size of the missile has its drawbacks, with larger naval craft unlikely to sustain much damage from a direct impact.

A Padasuri-6 missile is fired from its launcher during a test conducted in February 2024. Although capable of firing eight times the number of missiles as the Styx CDS, greatly increasing the chances of successfully penetrating a ship's defences, the launchers lack their own radar and rely on nearby coastal radar stations for target identification. (KCBC)

Kim Jong Un inspects an apparent (copy of a) Russian TRDD-50A engine in August 2023. (KCBC)

The new coastal defence complex armed with eight NLOS missiles. Thought to be capable of reaching targets up to 40 kilometres away, this system serves as an effective deterrent against amphibious landings and smaller naval vessels operating in proximity to the shore. (KCBC)

North Korea's NLOS missile is fired from a naval launcher, its fins still folded. The markings indicate that the canisters should be kept dry and upright, and are fragile. (KCBC)

With the Kumsong-3 and NLOS-capable missile providing much-needed modern firepower against lighter vessels, the legacy P-15 design with its heavy warhead was not entirely forgotten. Continued development leaning on the Chinese HY-2 and technologies such as those of the Exocet led to the introduction of a completely redesigned CDS in the late 1990s, according to some sources named the AG-1 (US DoD designation Serge) and first tested in 1997, but possibly as early as 1992.[5] Swapping its volatile propulsion system for a turbojet engine likely based on the French Microturbo TRI 60, it is capable of attaining ranges of up to 360 kilometres – a massive improvement over the oldest P-15 variants which have a range of 40 kilometres. Its launcher is typically based on the same chassis also used for many artillery systems of the early 1990s, although variants also exist that use the 323 APC chassis as a basis. In an effort to decrease the dependence on vulnerable static coastal defence radars, each launcher can operate autonomously using its own radar mounted in a box to the side of the vehicle to detect enemy targets. These launchers are backward compatible with the P-15 and its Chinese descendants, and are typically seen mounted with such older missiles during parades and exercises. The system was readily marketed abroad, and aside from being offered to Iraq, it was, ironically, exported to Iran in the early 2000s, which claims to produce the system itself under the designation Raad.[6] In expositions in this nation it has also been shown to use a modified seeker, showing some advances in this area although these upgrades were claimed to be indigenous by Iran. This claim is dubious given the fact that it has never produced this system. Since the missile associated with the system has actually never been spotted in North Korea itself, this claim is often held to be true however. Nevertheless, this CDS does indeed appear to be in use with the KPAN and is likely deployed in limited numbers on its east coast. Given the amount of technology that has become available since the introduction of the Raad, as the Iranians call it, it is highly likely that North Korea

Shore-based CDS like the 323-based example seen here are likely to have a significantly longer lifespan than the KPAN craft they are meant to support. The KPAN still mainly relies on older generation Styx-type descendants for its CDS, which are best used in combination with other AShMs or against vessels lacking appropriate countermeasures. (KCBC)

has continued to develop an even more advanced variant to this day to complement the Kumsong-3. Its most important characteristics would likely be a range that is once again much increased while retaining a heavy warhead, and incorporating many of the modern seeker and guidance technologies that have also been incorporated into the Kumsong-3. Such a system has never been displayed or mentioned in North Korean propaganda, but there is some indication that it was in fact first tested in July 2009 and received the US DoD designation of Scourge. It has a range of some 700 kilometres, putting the entire Korean Peninsula, much of the East Sea and even parts of Japan within range. Clearly, the DPRK was racing ahead with its cruise missile programmes in the early 2000s while much of the world was still coming to terms with the introduction of its Kh-35 derivatives.

Although much attention has been devoted to analysing the results of North Korea's indigenous development of Styx-type descendants, the most obvious clue to these exploits has been overlooked by many. First publicly showcased by its first export customer of Iran in 2007, the North Korean Serge CDS is capable of hitting targets up to 360km away, greatly improving upon the 40km and 200km range of the early P-15 and HY-2 whose technology it is based on. Building upon the successes obtained with the Serge, an AShM with an even longer range and possibly further improvements in its seeker design was first tested in 2009. Designated the Scourge by the US DoD, the 700km range of this missile is enough to target vessels underway in almost any part of the East Sea, making it likely that the missile was specifically designed with the threat of US carrier strike groups in mind. (Artwork by David Bocquelet)

And indeed, the beginning of the 2020s showed what North Korea had been working towards, with a September 2021 test of a new system first showing where their aspirations lay. The system in question consists of five massive elongated canisters on a single 4x4 transporter erector launcher (TEL), containing one of two types of cruise missiles. Exactly how these two types relate to one another is unclear, with both being showcased at separate displays at the Self-Defence-2021 exhibition in October 2021. State media coverage of a flurry of tests throughout 2022, 2023 and 2024 showed the systems to

What appears to be another strategic cruise missile launcher at the Self-Defence-2021 exhibition. Unlike other exhibits, the missile is not on display. Note the 76mm OTO Melara copy with RCS-reducing shape on the left. This cupola has currently only been observed installed on a single Tuman-class corvette. (KCBC)

be named Hwasal-1 ('Arrow-1') and Hwasal-2, though it remains uncertain which modifications to the paint scheme, guidance or engine typifies which variant. The most plausible theory currently seems to be that one constitutes a true AShM, whereas the other is a (nuclear-capable) land-attack cruise missile. Later tests added the Pulhwasal-3[7] to the family, which appears to be largely identical to earlier variants save for the fact that it is submarine-launched. Given that it can probably be deployed from the KPAN-standard 533mm torpedo tubes and can presumably carry a nuclear warhead, it notably broadens the available platforms to much of the KPA's submarine fleet, while the Hwasal-1 or 2 has meanwhile been deployed to several surface ships. Since various (Pul)Hwasal variants are believed to be a cornerstone of the DPRK's strategic deterrent however, this family will be discussed in more detail in the final volume of this series, which will cover the North's Missile General Bureau. The fact that the missile combines radar and optical guidance to accurately hit targets at up to 2,000 kilometres distance should serve to underline the fact that North Korean (anti-ship) cruise missile technology has matured to an advanced stage however. It would be a mistake to think that even this new system will spell the end of their ambitions, and yet another (even larger) cruise missile system first displayed during the 75th anniversary of the Workers' Party of Korea parade in 2020. Though scarce coverage of tests makes assessments of this system uncertain, it is believed to be responsible for firing Hwasal variants with supersized warheads.

A Hwasal-2 AShM is fired from its concealed launcher aboard an Amnok-class corvette during a test in August 2023. (KCBC)

A supersonic missile (as part of a volley of two) is launched during weapons tests on the destroyer *Choe Hyon* in April 2025. (KCBC)

The 'Haeil-2 Unmanned Underwater Nuclear Attack Boat' undergoing testing in April 2023. During the test, the UUV traversed waters off North Korea's east coast for more than 71 hours before its inert warhead was detonated. (KCBC)

Despite already constituting a diverse family of AShMs, the arsenal of available cruise missiles continued to grow throughout the 2020s, with a lack of known designations adding to the confusion surrounding the already opaque Hwasal family. Not one, but two new types of cruise missiles were seemingly demonstrated for the first time during weapons tests on the destroyer *Choe Hyon* in April 2025. Both types are believed to constitute downsized offshoots of the Hwasal family, with the more conventional of the two seeming largely similar to the Hwasal-1/2 except with a reduced diameter of some 450mm. The other is a more conspicuous deviation from existing technology, replacing the large warhead and seeker section with a tapered second stage equipped with guidance fins. According to state commentary, this allows the missile to attain supersonic speeds, greatly enhancing its chances against well-defended targets such as large naval ships. Presumably, this comes at the expense of reduced range, although neither the maximum speed or range are currently known. Both types are believed to be compatible with the VLS also used for known members of the Hwasal family; the reason for their reduced diameters as a result remains uncertain, and no other launch platforms have currently been unveiled. To further complicate matters, yet another new Hwasal variant was displayed during the 'Military Hardware Exhibition Defence Development-2025'. The missile in question bears a close resemblance to the Russian 3M54E (and, to a lesser degree, the Chinese JY-18E). While these AShMs are subsonic along much of their (sea-skimming) flight path, they feature a terminal supersonic sprint to evade ship-borne defences.

Aside from AShMs, the DPRK has also begun adopting alternative long-range assets to counter its opponents' navies. While there has long been speculation that some of its modern ballistic missiles could be adapted for an anti-ship ballistic-missile role, a much more obscure yet technologically mature option was shown to be in advanced stages of development in the 2020s. The so-called Haeil ('Tsunami') family of torpedo drones has likely been under development since as early as 2009, and meanwhile encompasses at least five types of differing sizes and capabilities. While there is likely to be some variety in guidance technology and intended use-cases, the Haeil family is primarily believed to be for strategic use, disabling ports, coastal targets and even naval formations using nuclear warheads. As such, it will be covered in more detail in the final volume of this series. Similarly, North Korea's new multirole destroyers feature VLS for eight Hwasong-11S ballistic missiles for ground strikes, whose precise characteristics will be explored to greater detail in the same volume.

Six members of the Hwasal family (with the new 3M54E lookalike fifth from the top) are displayed at the 'Military Hardware Exhibition Defence Development-2025'. The diversity of cruise missiles in North Korean service is now quickly surpassing that of most other nations. (KCBC)

Presumably, both the variety and size of North Korean VLS is to increase if its ambitions of constructing a cruiser come to fruition, mirroring the (now cancelled) South Korean Joint Strike Ship efforts in attempting to mate unprecedentedly large ballistic missiles to surface platforms.

One of the newest pieces of naval armament ironically appears to be rooted in positively antique equipment. Deriving from the Soviet OTA-40 (or newer TR-244), the quadruple torpedo launcher is believed to be around 400mm in calibre, and geared towards anti-submarine operations. This calibre was not previously known to be used by the KPAN, and it remains a possibility that the launcher was downsized to the readily available 324mm calibre. What torpedoes are compatible similarly remains

A display tent during the launch of the *Choe Hyon* in April 2025 showcases some of the newest armament available. On the right, a copy of the Pantsir-ME CIWS with 57E6M-E missile, an NLOS missile launcher in the back. At left, from front to back: an unidentified (ASW) missile, the 91RE1-like missile, a Kumsong-3, a member of the Hwasal family, the new small diameter cruise missile and the Hwasong-11S. (KCBC)

unknown: with the primary for the use for the system currently thought to be anti-submarine warfare. Simultaneously, two different types of anti-submarine missiles possibly carrying the same calibre torpedoes as payload were unveiled. While no tests have been disclosed yet and available footage is insufficient to make an accurate prediction of their characteristics, one of the types appears similar to the Russian 91RE1 Otvet, and may feature similar capabilities. In particular, they are believed to be compatible

with the same VLS that launch Hwasal-family missiles, thereby enhancing the versatility of any ships that don them. These types of munitions are by no means an end-all solution to the threat posed by South Korea's growing submarine fleet (let alone that of Japan or the US), and ASW activities will remain contingent on submarines' timely detection. Be that as it may, the era where North Korea's ASW efforts amounted to little more than perfunctory of dubious efficacy is clearly soon to be over.

5

SURFACE EFFECT SHIPS

The array of newly available weapons technologies would be pioneered on what was another highly unique approach to shipbuilding undertaken by the DPRK. Started sometime in the 1990s with the production of a series of unique fast watercraft prototypes, these highly specialised ships use a twin-hulled design as well as an air cushion to create a layer of air underneath their body, enabling them to glide over the water at very high speeds with only a small portion of the hull submerged. This type of craft, known as a surface effect ship (SES), would also be the first to introduce the concept of stealth to a large KPAN naval vessel, dividing the class into a line of regular SES combatants and their radar-reducing stealth SES descendants. The North Korean design is optimised for high-speed coastal operations but can also be used on the open sea to engage larger adversaries.

The first type in this class, henceforth referred to as SES I (part of a broader class referred to as the Nongo by the US DoD), was constructed in the mid or late 1990s at Nampho harbour and measured about 37 metres in length. As only a single ship was produced, presumably to investigate the feasibility of the SES design, its armament was a hodgepodge of both the newest systems available to the DPRK as well as some of its most outdated ones. Perhaps the most important introduction of weaponry on this craft was North

Korea's own variant of the Soviet 30mm AK-630 CIWS, for which no suitable radars appear to be present on SES I. It can therefore only be operated manually via a separate aiming station using iron sights, severely limiting its effective range and combat value. The vessel is outfitted with two of these systems, one on the bow and one near the aft of the vessel, the manual aiming stations of which are located on two elevated round platforms next to the bridge, above the rear of the ship's two AShMs.[1] These AShMs consist of the ubiquitous Soviet-legacy Styx-type descendants, although the similarity between the original Soviet variants, their Chinese copies and upgrades and North Korea's indigenously redesigned missiles makes it extremely difficult to determine which are used on SES I. Other weaponry consists of two blocks of 4x6 107mm MRLs on the bow, which appear to have been automated and operated from the bridge. Still, its radar suite is limited, using a Japanese Furuno radar for navigation and what appears to be a surface search radar similar in design to the MR-331, as seen on the Komar- and Osa I-class. Underlining the prototypical nature of this craft, only one was ever produced, which appears to have entered service with KPAN Unit 189 at Pipagot naval base in 2005 or 2006 after years of trials. However, it returned to Nampho in the late 2010s, and even at Pipagot it spent most of its time laid bare well away from the main port.

A view from the rear of SES I. Note its bulky AShM launchers, and indigenous AK-630-derived aft CIWS. (KCBC)

Another shot of the same vessel during a visit by Kim Jong Il. Note the two elevated round platforms for manual aiming stations (or alternatively: MANPADS) (KCBC)

Development of this type of craft continued and bore fruit in what will be referred to here as SES IIa by the late 1990s. Although largely identical in hull shape and size at 37 metres long and 12 metres wide, the weaponry and radar suite was radically altered to incorporate many of the KPAN's most advanced technologies at the time. One surprising new weapon system that it premiered was the indigenous copy of the Italian 76mm OTO Melara naval artillery system. Since this cannon requires a sizeable revolving magazine below decks, it cannot be mounted on all ships and SES IIa's internal hull plan must differ significantly from that of SES I. Additionally, it mounts the North's indigenously designed fire-control radar for guidance, and another radar closely resembling the Chinese Type 362 which is responsible for threat detection and navigation. Interestingly, a manual aiming station in front of the bridge is slaved to this system, providing whoever wields it with an obscene amount of firepower.[2] To provide cover for the rear of the vessel one indigenous AK-630 CIWS copy was placed abaft, this time slaved to a Soviet MR-104 Drum Tilt radar mounted behind the bridge, without which the system had significantly less operational value. Additionally, one of the new short-range SAM stations was mounted between the Drum Tilt radar and the AK-630 copy. Although both this SAM system and the AK-630 have roughly the same maximum range at five kilometres, though

a lower effective range, the combination of these two systems represents a reasonably capable close-in defence capability, especially when combined with the heavier 76mm OTO Melara copy. However, despite representing some of the newest emerging technologies within the KPAN, by far the most important and innovative weaponry introduced on SES IIa were its AShMs. Eight Kumsong-3 missile tubes are mounted on two racks beside the bridge, replacing the two Styx-type descendants seen on SES I and thereby greatly expanding its anti-ship capabilities.

Although only two vessels in the SES IIa-class were ever produced, another SES with the same dimensions and weaponry, but updated radar systems, was manufactured in the mid to late 2000s at Nampho harbour. This craft, designated SES IIb from here on, replaces the indigenous fire-control radar of the OTO Melara and Type 362 with radomes presumably containing improved equipment. The MR-104 Drum Tilt was likely retained however, so the primary weaponry that benefits from the enhanced radar suite are the 76mm OTO Melara and North Korean Kh-35 derivatives. Since these AShMs are largely dependent on the ability to detect their targets at long ranges as a limiting factor, an improved radar can greatly add to their capabilities. Aside from the improvements to the radar suite no further modifications are apparent, and despite the supposed capabilities of SES IIb, no other craft of this type have as of yet been produced, possibly due to the development of more advanced replacements.

Parallel to the regular SES programme initiated on the west coast during the 1990s, another project was started during the same period on the other side of the country, looking to bring modern ideas such as low radar cross-section (RCS) and other stealth features to the SES concept. This led to a first 'stealth SES' prototype in the late 1990s, which will henceforth be referred to as SSES Ia, part of a broader class referred to as the Haesam by the US DoD. This craft, measuring some 38 metres long and 13 metres wide, was likely designed with the primary purpose of testing whether the stealth SES concept was feasible in mind, and featured little in the way of armament and radar suite. Although the scarce footage and information available render it difficult to form any hard conclusions about the design, it appears to have been outfitted with a frontal cannon in a stealthily shaped cupola and either carried the regular AK-230 or North Korea's AK-630 derivative based in the same turret on its aft. A single image purporting to show this elusive first prototype exists, and although its authenticity cannot be verified it appears to match with satellite imagery, possibly indicating that SSES Ia is outfitted with no radars whatsoever, meaning that its armament could well consist of mere mock-ups. The hull itself had already for a large part taken the typical shape that would exemplify future SSES designs however, with sharply angled features and sloped surfaces giving it a characteristically stealthy look.

A SES IIa in Nampho harbour in 2018. (KCBC)

The only publicly known image of the SSES Ia before its conversion to its current layout. Although it matches the vagueness of images purporting to show the Loch Ness Monster, the silhouette clearly shows the main gun mounted in a stealthily shaped cupola and what appears to an indigenous AK-630 copy on the rear deck. (Authors' archive)

a flat 'travel' mode and erect 'launch' mode. A small mast has been fitted atop the bridge to provide rudimentary radar capabilities, with the primary radars consisting of one Japanese Furuno radome radar sensor and two open radar sensors of the same brand.[3] Short-range air-defence (SHORAD) is provided by two of the North's indigenous AK-630 CIWS derivatives placed on the ship's fore and rear decks, and the short-range SAM station also seen on SES II, is mounted between the rear CIWS and the bridge. Due to a lack of more powerful radars capable of guiding this weaponry, the indigenous AK-630s are directed manually through two remote aiming stations located shortly in front of and on top of the bridge. A third remote aiming station is also present on the bridge, the purposes of which are not entirely certain but which might be slaved to both CIWS at the same time. Additionally, four 14.5mm six-barrelled rotary machine gun stations were mounted on the hull, two beside the front of the bridge and two beside the aft AK-630 derivative.

Despite its prototypical nature, the hull of SSES Ia was preserved and subsequently used as a basis for the first SSES that would become operational, which we will designate SSES Ib here. Converted sometime in the mid 2000s, this redeveloped naval craft with hull number 9201 was likely created in order to test emergent technologies such as the Kumsong-3 AShM on this new platform, in the process completely negating most of the ship's previously stealthy aspects. In order to enable the original hull to carry these missiles, for which it was obviously not designed, the midsection was broadened slightly aft of the bridge, making room for two launchers each carrying two canisters, with the option for mounting two more for a total of eight. Due to the sloped hull, this did not in fact increase the vessel's width. Foreshadowing the way these missiles would be fitted to later variants in the SSES line, the launchers feature a hydraulic mechanism allowing the canisters to be switched between

SSES Ib during tests of its Kumsong-3 AShMs. The trainable AShM racks can likely carry another four launch tubes, for a total of eight missiles on a single craft. (KCBC)

A Kumsong-3 AShM is fired from the deck of SSES Ib. North Korea's AK-630 CIWS copy and two 14.5mm rotary machine guns can be seen in front. (KCBC)

Underlining the prototypical nature of the SES I, its armament was a hodgepodge of systems not particularly well-suited to the role of a modern fast attack craft. Equipped with just two AShMs, two manually-aimed 30mm AK-630 copies and interestingly, two multiple rocket launchers for unguided rockets of 107mm calibre, its equipment is a clear reflection of the lack of modern weaponry and technology faced by the KPAN until the mid 1990s. Despite the emergence of more modern weaponry fitted to later ships in the SES series, the SES I continues to operate in its original configuration. (Artwork by Anderson Subtil)

The SES series reached its maturity with the development of the SES IIa, a vessel that is outwardly similar to the SES I but in fact incorporates some of the KPAN's most advanced technologies at the time, including a radar-guided 76mm OTO Melara copy, one indigenous AK-630 CIWS copy slaved to a Soviet MR-104 Drum Tilt radar and a MANPADS station on the rear of the ship. Although these do much to increase the craft's survivability against AShMs and aircraft, the most important introduction of weaponry on this craft are the eight Kumsong-3 AShMs mounted beside the bridge: a steep improvement over the SES I's two Styx-type descendants. (Artwork by Anderson Subtil)

Identical to the SES IIa in layout and armament, the SES IIb brings with it an expanded radar housed in large radomes. Since fast attack craft are largely dependent on the ability to detect their targets at large ranges, an improved radar could greatly increase the lethality of the Kumsong-3 AShMs carried onboard. Nevertheless SES IIb would be the only ship to be outfitted with this expanded radar suite, with later generations of SES craft settling on a more simplistic radar suite built around Japanese Furuno radars, presumably due to cost restraints and stealth considerations. (Artwork by Anderson Subtil)

The SSES I was likely designed with the primary purpose of testing whether the stealth SES concept was feasible, after which it was converted to a test bed for a new type of AShM launcher featuring a hydraulic erection mechanism, which would also be its final operational configuration. Outfitted with a MANPADS station and six rotary cannons of calibres 14.5mm and 30mm, a lack of suitable radars greatly limits its combat effectiveness. Therefore, the SSES I's value as a test platform might well exceed its actual combat value. (Artwork by Anderson Subtil)

The next development in the stealth SES series made a first attempt at incorporating low-observable properties into an operational design. Opposed to the arrangement of the AShMs on previous SES craft and indeed on most fast attack craft, the Kumsong-3 AShMs on the SSES II have been fitted in two internal hull compartments on a hydraulic erection mechanism. Nevertheless, the choice of secondary armament does away with much of the RCS-reducing properties, making the choice for internal hull compartments an innovative but useless design decision. Interestingly, although it lacks a guidance radar for the AK-630 copy, the SSES II is fitted with two MANPADS stations with six missiles ready to fire each. (Artwork by Anderson Subtil)

The ultimate development of the (stealth) SES line is the most well-armed fast attack craft in the history of the KPAN. Potentially capable of carrying 16 Kumsong-3 AShMs (or a comparable outfit of other modern types) fitted in four internal hull compartments, the SSES III carries the same number of missiles as eight Komar/Sohung-class fast attack craft. It is also the first stealth SES likely to be fitted with a fire-control radar for the AK-630 copy located on the aft, which greatly improves upon the ship's defences against enemy AShMs and aircraft. As the construction of the SSES III was still ongoing at the time of publication of this book, details might differ from what can be seen in the artwork. (Artwork by Anderson Subtil)

The next development along the stealth SES line, referred to as SSES II in this chapter, would include a radical new feature to regain some of its stealthy features lost on SSES Ib. To allow for this new feature the length of the design was increased to roughly 41 metres, although many other aspects of the craft, such as its width and the angular design of the hull and bridge, were preserved. The Kumsong-3 missiles, until now rather bluntly mounted to the exterior of the hull, have been fitted in two internal hull compartments on a hydraulic erection mechanism similar to the one tested on SSES Ib, meaning that the new stealth SES design is capable of traversing the seas in 'stealth mode' and will only break the smooth lines of its low-observable design when it is about to fire one of its AShMs. This feature causes SSES II to be remarkably similar to the Norwegian Skjold-class stealth SES, a corvette of which six entered service with the Royal Norwegian Navy in the 2010s, and which has comparable dimensions as well as the capability to fire eight anti-ship missiles from compartments embedded in its hull. To further complete the analogy, SESS II is also outfitted with the North Korean 76mm OTO Melara derivative, albeit without the RCS-reducing cupola that the Skjold-class's more advanced Otobreda 76/62 Super Rapid has. The number of AShMs carried in SSES II's internal hull compartments is not confirmed; although the hull's dimensions should allow for fitting four canisters in either compartment for a total of eight missiles, the fact that SSES Ib was seen carrying only two canisters on each launcher might imply the total number of missiles is four. Despite the RCS-reducing properties of the new AShM compartments, the choice of secondary armament once again heavily disrupts its smooth lines and negates most of the advantages gained in this area. Two SAM stations and two manually-aimed 14.5mm rotary machine gun stations complement the 76mm mounted near the bow and a North Korean AK-630 derivative mounted aft of the bridge. This turret had to be placed on a raised platform in order to be able to fire in a 360 degree arc, which would otherwise have been encumbered by the two 14.5mm rotary machine gun stations tightly fitted around it, a result of the reduced space available now that most of the aft of the hull contains AShM launchers. Neither the 76mm or 30mm systems are automated, and no fire-control systems are present on SSES II. Instead, the bridge houses two manual aiming stations, relegating both pieces of powerful weaponry almost completely unusable against fast moving or distant targets. The radar mast has been fortified and increased in size compared to SSES I however, and houses several Furuno radars as well as what might be two forward-looking infrared (FLIR) pods. An extensive redesign of the bridge itself is most noticeable in that its aft has been narrowed and its overall height increased. Although it was nearing completion in 2009, it continued to be laid bare and tested at the facility where it was constructed in Wonsan until mid 2016, only entering service in the same unit as SSES I later that year. Whether the reason behind this was some unforeseen complication in its design or simply because it was still prototypical in nature is uncertain.

The ultimate development in the stealth SES line took place in recent years on the opposite coast: SSES III has been under construction in Nampho harbour since late 2012. Although the first half of its twin hull was laid down in early October 2012, assembly was still ongoing halfway through September 2014 after which progress on the craft became obscured by a newly erected shelter.

A look at the rear of the sole SSES II vessel to have entered service. Its Kumsong-3 AShMs are well hidden in the internal hull compartments of the vessel. (KCBC)

SSES III brings with it another increase in hull length to around 43 metres, which is a direct result of its most significant improvement over SSES II; the rear now accommodates four separate launchers in internal hull compartments. As each of these is potentially capable of carrying four Kumsong-3 AShMs, this could give SSES III the impressive number of 16 missiles to unleash on its opponents. Since the effectiveness of AShMs in a countermeasure-rich environment is often directly related to the number of missiles fired at once, this greatly increases its capabilities against modern foes. The additional launchers have resulted in a rearrangement of the rear deck, which will likely carry a single North Korean AK-630 derivative towards the aft, which due to the lack of 14.5mm weapon stations would no longer require the platform seen on SSES II, and a SAM system between that and the bridge. The bridge itself was left largely unmodified compared to SSES II aside from the addition of a lower platform which is likely used to house the fire-control radar of the AK-630 copy. Forward armament once again consists of a 76mm OTO Melara (presumably now with a stealthily angled cupola), and possibly two manually-aimed 14.5mm rotary machine gun stations. Indeed, with up to 16 Kumsong-3 missiles the only limiting factor on its capabilities as a 'carrier killer' is the ship's ability to detect its targets, so heavy investment in the procurement and development of suitable radars for SSES III would be a sensible course of action for the KPAN.[4] However, considering the similarity in weaponry on board and general layout of the bridge, the radars seen on SSES II would be a solid match for SSES III. Development of SSES III has been incredibly protracted, and the vessel was brought out of its workshop only in October 2022, a full decade after construction

began.[5] Before it is actually commissioned into the KPAN another lengthy period of some testing but mostly inactivity will undoubtedly follow.

In the meantime, another SES that appears to combine elements of both its stealthy and conventional predecessors has begun construction, with a hull first appearing in satellite imagery in Nampho in 2018 which had the same dimensions and general layout as that of SES II. Though ostensibly less ambitious than SSES III, this tentative SSES IV seems to suffer from a lack of weaponry and other equipment to outfit the bare hull, which has lain bare since its initial sighting. Therefore, little about its characteristics can be stated other than that it is likely destined to receive a 76mm OTO Melara copy, 30mm AK-630 copy and two hull-embedded Kumsong-3 launchers as its main armament. Ironically, the more muted approach to its design compared to SSES III might well have been an attempt to find a balance that was ready for large-scale production, a prospect that now seems implausible. The fact that stealth SESs are now apparently being produced on both coasts seemingly suggested an ambitious production plan for additional craft. However, it remains to be seen whether any kind of serial production will actually ever commence, and at the current rate of assembly, which has seen eight SESs partially completed in a quarter century, a significant deployment of these vessels remains a relatively distant threat. Even if serial production picks up, the fact that many older KPAN craft are simultaneously being upgraded and produced implies that the SES classes are to supplement rather than replace existing ships, which means that the total number produced in the foreseeable future may remain low indeed.

6

LARGE SHIP CONSTRUCTION

Large ship construction, while virtually non-existent in the years after the creation of the Soho-class, has seen a significant revival in the 2010s and 2020s. However, the first indication that the DPRK's ambitions towards introducing large naval vessels had not abated came during the early 2000s, when a stripped Project 11351 Nerei 'Krivak III-class' frigate arrived in Wonsan harbour. This ship, commissioned into the Maritime Border Guard of the KGB at the end of 1987 under the name *Imeni 70-Letiya VChk-KGB* (renamed *Pskov* in 1991), was moved to Avacha Bay on the Kamchatka Peninsula on 26 October 2002 in order to be dismantled to a point where it could be sold for scrap, and was supposedly carried off to China to be scrapped on 28 February 2003. However, it instead popped up in Wonsan harbour soon after, and was spotted in Nampho harbour in January 2004. Rather than scrapping the hull, North Korea soon began work on bringing the ship back to operational condition. The proposed armament of the ship as detailed on a model located in the MPAF revolutionary museum in Pyongyang incorporated several of the North's AK-630 copies directed by MR-104 Drum Tilts, one casemated 100mm gun and several 25mm 2M-3 anti-aircraft guns. The design also included two quad-canister Kumsong-3 launchers installed on either side of the bridge in a similar fashion to that of the Russian Project 1155 Udaloy-class, instead of the more conventional crosswise installation midships. Also of interest is the fact that the ship's helicopter deck apparently would not have been retained, instead making room for more weapon systems and other

equipment. Although work on the hull had commenced shortly after its arrival in Nampho, virtually no progress in overhauling the ship was booked between late 2004 and late 2006. The fact that the ship could no longer be seen in subsequent satellite imagery confirmed that the project had been too ambitious for the DPRK. Whether due to the lack of availability of suitable heavy weaponry, the fact that all (military) equipment had been removed prior to its arrival in the DPRK, or simply because the work and materiel needed proved to be too demanding for North's shipbuilding industry, the programme would never be completed. Almost half a decade after it had originally been scheduled to be scrapped, the hull was finally dismantled sometime between late 2006 and early 2008. Nonetheless, the experience gained while designing and planning for the overhaul of this ship, at 123 metres the longest military craft to be commissioned for the KPAN, will ultimately surely have proven to be invaluable in its future endeavours towards large shipbuilding.

The next project came to be after an unofficial revival of ties between Myanmar and North Korea during the early 2000s, which saw North Korean technicians working on a variety of military projects for Myanmar inside the country. Although their presence is often linked to a possible nuclear weapons programme as well as building hardened infrastructure for sensitive military installations, the most tangible manifestation of North Korean influence in today's Tatmadaw (Myanmar's Armed Forces) comes in the form of their first frigate: the F11 *Aung Zeya*. This naval craft, measuring 108 metres long, was

The *Imeni 70-Letiya VChk-KGB* seen here 15 years before its transfer to North Korea. Having been stripped of any useful (military) equipment, to bring the ship back to operational condition ultimately proved too ambitious for the DPRK. (United States Navy)

laid down in 2008 and completed in 2011. With the DPRK supplying the design, weaponry and part of the radar suite as well as providing technical supervision, the F11 was essentially the first North Korean-produced frigate after the Soho-class, and the first successful one after the Najin-class. As described in leaked files regarding a visit from a delegation of Burmese defence officials to the DPRK in November 2008, the 'Nam Po Ship Design and Institute Office' marketed a 2,500 tonne class measuring 108 by 13.3 metres and carrying a range of weaponry produced in North Korea, which closely matches the frigate built in Myanmar.[1] Specifically, the sighting of two launchers carrying Kumsong-3 AShMs midships was the first indication that these missiles were being made in the DPRK, and were apparently even exported as early as the mid 2000s. Since the Kumsong-3 became known to the public only in June 2014, the fact that they had been operational for at least a decade at that point is remarkable. Nonetheless, considering the introduction of the Kumsong-3 capable SES IIa by the turn of the millennium this should not have been too surprising. The fact that these missiles were exported in general shows the willingness of North Korea to bring its most advanced weaponry to the market, and is an important factor to consider in estimating their ability to produce complicated systems in the twenty-first century.

Other North Korean-produced weapon systems installed on this helicopter-capable vessel include four of the North's 30mm CIWS, two 14.5mm rotary machine guns, one MANPADS-based SAM station, two 252mm RBU-1200 anti-submarine launchers (of a modified trainable design, permitting them to be aimed separately from the ship itself) and a number of the 82mm smoke/chaff launchers. The radar suite includes Japanese Furuno radars, a North Korean copy of the Chinese Type 362 search radar, and three fire-control systems (FCS) of indigenous North Korean manufacture that direct the gun systems. Nonetheless, part of the ship's equipment was sourced from other nations, such as a sonar system and the RAWL long-range search radar which were acquired from India as North Korea was unable to provide comparable equipment, as well as the 76mm

OTO Melara which Myanmar purchased from Israel, even though North Korea does produce the system itself. Various minor upgrades performed later, such as the installation of a special RCS-reducing cupola for the OTO Melara, were performed by Myanmar on its own and likely have no connection to the DPRK. Despite being marketed abroad, none of these impressive ships were built for indigenous use and the vessels that would thereafter materialise in the DPRK itself would actually be corvettes rather than full-size frigates.

The 2010s would bring a comparatively successful indigenous programme that called for the construction of four new large naval combatants, setting the stage for a renewal of the naval power competition between North and South on the conventional front. Although progress on the new corvettes, two of which have been under assembly at either coast since late 2011, has generally been slow and disorderly, they appear to be poised to finally all be commissioned into the KPAN in the mid 2020s. At a length of 77 metres each, the new vessels constituted the largest naval project undertaken by the DPRK in decades, bringing new capabilities to the table that smaller craft are unable to provide. The two vessels that were the first to be laid at Rajin and Nampho apparently received the US DoD designation of Tuman-class and were completed in 2013.[2] These two vessels were presumably intended to function

The F11 *Aung Zeya* underway. (Tatmadaw – Myawaddy TV)

The crosswise-installed quad canisters for the Kumsong-3 on the F11 *Aung Zeya*. The *Aung Zeya* is the only Myanmarese ship that carries the Kumsong-3 AShM. (Tatmadaw – Myawaddy TV)

Outfitting of the east coast Amnok-class corvette in August 2016, with only the main gun still missing. Note the open torpedo hatch towards the aft. (NK Pro)

as support ships, and featured a very large helicopter deck which could carry either a Mi-14 or Ka-28 helicopter for ASW missions. However, their sole armament consisted of four 252mm anti-submarine rocket launchers on the fore deck, and the radar suite was similarly limited, comprising just two Japanese Furuno radars and a copy of the Chinese Type 362 search radar. This, combined with a layout perhaps more suited to a leisure craft, apparently resulted in a dissatisfactory end product, and in mid 2014 work began on reconstructing the Nampho-based helicopter-capable corvette into a proper warship, with the Rajin example following suit in 2017.

The vessels that these ships were meant to support were in the meantime taking a lot longer to construct, entering service in 2017 and designated the Amnok-class by the US DoD.[3] Heavily armed and outfitted with RCS-reducing features, these ships are the culmination of over two decades of experiments with new naval warfare concepts, and a clear indication of the direction in which North Korean shipbuilding is heading. After their refitting, the two Tuman-class ships now closely resemble the Amnok-class save for less weaponry and most notably the design of the bridge, and likely are not dissimilar in their capabilities. Their primary armament consists of two AShM launchers, which are fitted in internal compartments so as not to compromise the RCS-reducing features of the ship. These were initially believed to be destined solely for Kumsong-3s, but with the ships' protracted outfitting and rapid developments in missile technology, the Hwasal-1 or Hwasal-2 was shown to have substituted (or possibly complemented) the type instead during a

The east coast Tuman-class corvette berthed in Rajin, April 2016. In its original configuration the corvette looks more like an oversized private yacht than an actual warship. Like the Soho-class frigate and the North Korean-designed frigate *Aung Zeya*, the Tuman-class corvettes featured a much larger helicopter deck than found on comparable ships elsewhere. Nonetheless, there is space for only one helicopter and no hangar is present. (NK Pro)

The east coast Amnok-class corvette 'Patrol Ship No. 661' underway. The vessel still carries a 100mm gun instead of the 76mm OTO Melara system installed on the west coast Amnok-class corvette, though it is likely to receive this system eventually. (KCBC)

live firing in August 2023. This effects a shift in their capabilities as well as overall role, with long-range land attacks and even tactical nuclear strikes now in their purview. For all their modern features, only the west coast Amnok and Tuman-class ships seem to use the 76mm OTO Melara copy, with the east coast examples instead relying on a manually loaded 100mm cannon reminiscent of those found on North Korean gunboats from the 1980s. The reason for the peculiar omission of modern technology in this aspect is uncertain, but it is possible that the 76mm is simply too difficult to produce in significant numbers for the moment and therefore supplemented with legacy weaponry. This theory is supported by the fact that the cannons on these ships have been removed and reinstalled many times, with the Tuman-class ships even going without for years on end. Aside from a Drum Tilt in front of the main mast presumably tasked with guiding the main armament, another Drum Tilt

situated atop the AShM compartments provides fire-control for the two AK-630 copies which are placed on its rear decks. What appears to be a manual aiming station is located behind the AShM compartments which controls both CIWS, another in front of the bridge is seemingly slaved to the 76mm OTO Melara copy on the west coast corvettes, while serving as a backup for the corvettes on the east coast until they too are equipped with the OTO Melara copy. Complementing the Amnoks' CIWS is a MANPADS-based SAM system mounted on the rear deck, which for lack of space does not appear to be present on the Tuman-class. Likewise, two manually operated 14.5mm rotary machine gun emplacements in front of the Amnok-class's bridge provide additional firepower against small naval targets or slow-flying aerial targets. Ancillary systems include 82mm decoy launchers as well as four 252mm anti-submarine rocket launchers on the front deck, and the radar suite includes the same Japanese Furuno radars and Chinese Type 362 search radars originally fitted to the Tuman-class, in addition to an Osa-class-legacy Nikhrom-RRM antenna and an EO device. Another curious design feature is embedded in the rear hull of the ship: two torpedo launchers carrying two torpedoes each can be rotated outward to provide a short-range supplement to its AShMs. Equipping a large and modern naval craft with torpedoes is quite unconventional, and the fact that North Korea has deemed it to be prudent might indicate it has obtained an advanced torpedo design, such as the VA-111 Shkval supercavitating torpedo also in use with Iran. Torpedo tubes could also be used to deploy so-called uncrewed underwater vessels (UUVs), in the form of remote operated suicide attack craft typically shaped like torpedoes. While there is no clear indication that North Korea operates such vessels (aside nuclear-armed variants), traditional allies like Iran do, and state media reports in 2024 referred to Kim Jong Un's calls for 'developing not only underwater strategic weapon systems like a nuclear torpedo but also various types of unmanned underwater suicide attack craft'.[4]

A view of the 76mm OTO Melara copy mounted in an angular turret installed on the Tuman-class corvette stationed along the west coast. Its fire rate was clocked at approximately 95 rounds per minute. (KCBC)

The Najin-class frigates remain some of the North's largest sea-going vessels, and the west coast example shown here has been upgraded in the 2010s to incorporate some of the weaponry that has become available in the past decades. The upgrades stopped short of truly modernising the vessel however, and much of its original armament including its AK-230 CIWS is still present. New additions include two racks for the Kumsong-3 AShM, four torpedo tubes towards the aft, a MANPADS station and a Furuno radar for navigation. Unlike on other refurbished craft, no 14.5mm rotary machine guns were added, and the original 25mm 2M3s were retained instead. (Artwork by Anderson Subtil)

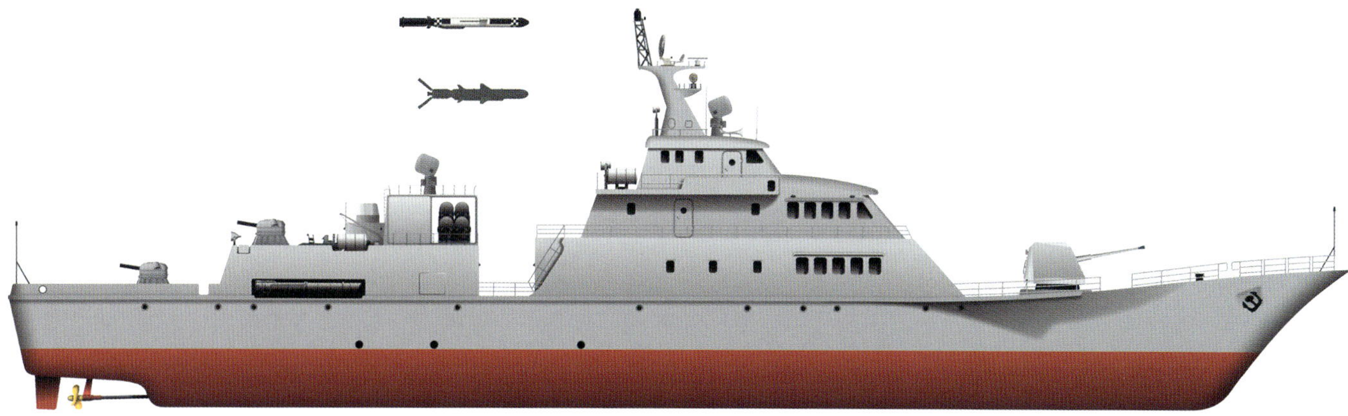

The two Tuman-class helicopter corvettes were rebuilt to largely the same template as the Amnok-class, but with obvious differences arising from the peculiarities of their original design. Most immediately obvious is the fact that the bridge of the original Tuman-class variant was retained, thus creating a somewhat odd look for a modern warship. Since it was also larger, the fore 14.5mm rotary machine guns, the short-range SAM and RBU-1200s of the Amnok-class could not be fitted. Nonetheless, its warfighting capabilities are largely identical to its sister ships in other regards. Displayed is the west coast Tuman-class corvette fitted with a copy of the 76mm OTO Melara housed in an angular turret. (Artwork by Anderson Subtil)

The west coast Amnok-class 77-metre long corvette. Note the radar cross-section reducing features such as its stealthy angles and internal compartments for its AShMs and torpedoes. Armament consists of two 30mm AK-630 copies to the rear, as well as MANPADS-based SAM station for SHORAD. A 76mm OTO Melara copy, 14.5mm rotary machine gun stations and four RBU-1200 anti-submarine rocket launchers complete its weapons suite, and two MR-104 Drum Tilt radars are used for guidance, apart from separate navigational and surface search radars. (Artwork by Anderson Subtil)

While development in typical North Korean fashion has taken its fair time, and some of the vessels are still being worked on even in 2024, the four new warships are now set to join a fleet which has in the 2000s and 2010s seen an accelerated pace of modernisation and renewed optimism in its future. Naval vessels like the Amnok- and Tuman-class still have little chance of facing off against larger naval combatants of the ROKN and US Navy, especially given the limited number produced so far, but they can function as a force multiplier amongst a range of smaller new classes entering service.

They provide the range and heavy firepower other vessels struggle to deliver, and above all tie together the KPAN's scattered units around a single core. Given the vigour with which new designs were being introduced one might have been forgiven for thinking these four ships were just the vanguard of a more extensive production programme. Yet by the early 2020s, the momentum of the KPAN's modernisation drive seemed to have been lost, with projects mainly lying dormant and awaiting outfitting. However, the lack of observed progress might be explained by a change of priorities in shipbuilding behind the scenes, with Kim Jong Un stressing the importance of greater KPAN involvement in the overall strategies and operations of the KPA in 2023.[5] This refrain was repeated during 2024 visits to Nampho as well as the massive naval base being constructed near Munchon since about 2015, during which the leader reportedly discussed 'a new huge plan [in shipbuilding]' and that they were 'soon to possess large surface warships and submarines which cannot be anchored at the existing facilities'.[6, 7]

Actual construction of the new class commenced at Nampho in February 2024, and progressed at breakneck speed.[8, 9] Since no shipbuilding facilities large enough to conceal the vessel were available, a new construction hall was progressively erected around the ship even as its hull was laid down. Though this gradually obscured it from satellite photography thus making estimations of its dimensions and tonnage difficult, images broadcast on state TV later that year cast some light on the specifications involved. Measuring in at approximately 142 metres in length and with a beam of some 16 metres, the warship is undeniably the largest and most ambitious shipbuilding project undertaken by the country yet, and may comfortably be called a frigate. With a stated displacement of 5,000 tonnes and a crew complement of 253, it is projected to be a true 'blue water' vessel, perhaps the first North Korean ship that can confidently claim such status. The ship was launched on 25 April 2025, and christened the *Choe Hyon*, the first of the eponymous Choe Hyon-class multirole destroyers.[10] And indeed, while the vessel's size and displacement straddle the line between frigate and destroyer, its heavy missile armament probably warrants its classification in the latter category. Most conspicuous are large sections of hull space in front of the bridge and stern reserved for 74 VLS cells of four different sizes, permitting the ship extensive anti-air, anti-ship, anti-submarine and land-attack capabilities. Combined with other launch cells, upwards of 106 missiles of at least 10 different types are believed to be carried at the ready. These notably include the first substantial missile-based air-defence capabilities for any

KPAN asset. Twenty VLS cells (12 on the front deck and eight astern) are fitted with Pyoljji-1 long-range SAMs (presumably both variants), with four large phased array radars embedded in the upper segment of the bridge serving as acquisition and guidance systems. Thirty-two smaller VLS cells on the front deck are believed to be reserved for Pyoljji-3 missiles, providing a robust SHORAD capability. These already substantial capabilities are paired with a copy of the Russian Pantsir-ME CIWS aft of the exhaust stack, whose hypersonic 57E6M-E missiles provide a degree of protection against higher velocity threats. Two copies of the AK-630 midships (guided by new phased array radars) as well as two 14.5mm rotary cannons concealed behind panelling on either side round off close-in defences (apart from at least 10 pintle-mounted 14.5mm KPVs distributed across the ship's various decks). On the offensive side, the front deck prominently features a copy of the 127mm OTO 127/64 LW long-range naval gun, which in its original form can be used in both an anti-ship and anti-air role depending on the munitions employed. For land-attack purposes, eight very large VLS containing Hwasong-11S short-range ballistic missiles are situated towards the stern. These could be utilised to extend the range of North Korea's ballistic missile arsenal to whatever theatre it hopes to project force in in the future. However, the possibility of fitting nuclear warheads means the warship is also afforded a strategic role (as also attested by state media coverage) – in which configuration the Hwasong-11S might also be effective against enemy fleet concentrations. A further 12 VLS (situated in between those of the Hwasong-11S and the aft Pyoljji-1) are believed to be reserved for various offshoots of the Hwasal family of cruise missiles fitted with gas generators to allow for cold launch. These include both regular diameter Hwasal cruise missiles and their new smaller diameter variants, which include a supersonic type as well as two anti-submarine variants.[11] For smaller land targets and naval craft, two quadruple NLOS launchers are available astride the exhaust stack. Its anti-ship capabilities are further supplemented by a canted compartment midships (similar to those

A top view of the destroyer *Choe Hyon* during its launch in April 2025, showing its prominent bridge, front VLS, and 127mm naval gun. (KCBC)

Another shot of the destroyer's rear, with the helicopter/drone deck in full view, as well as the aft VLS, Pantsir-ME CIWS copy and adjacent exhaust stack. (KCBC)

In this view from the waterfront, the destroyer's radar masts and prominent bridge with embedded phased array radars are at full display. (KCBC)

found on the Tuman and Amnok-class) which is likely reserved for eight Kumsong-3 AShMs. Another feature also found on the new corvettes are its concealed dual 533mm torpedo launchers, for a total of four torpedoes of unknown design ready to launch (potentially including one of the anti-submarine missiles). More curious is a second set of hidden torpedo launchers, located abaft from the first, believed to be of a quadruple 400mm ASW-configured design not yet known to be in KPAN service. The trainable RBU-1200-based anti-submarine rocket launchers also present on the Amnok and modified Tuman-class ships are also present, albeit hidden from view behind panelling in the bridge, presumably to maintain a measure of radar stealth. The legacy 82mm chaff/smoke launchers have meanwhile been replaced by four turreted systems surrounding the Pantsir-ME copy sporting 40 tubes each, whose movement like other weapons systems has presumably been fully automated. While a sizeable helicopter deck is present at the stern of the destroyer, two small adjacent hangar doors appear to suggest it is intended for use not by helicopters but by drones. Drone operations would afford yet another degree of flexibility to the ship, especially in terms of reconnaissance and surveillance missions.

The structure of the ship itself also warrants closer examination. Two large masts atop the bridge and exhaust stack extend the height of its silhouette from afar, carrying a number of radar systems not yet seen on other vessels. The imported Furuno radars of older vessels have been replaced by larger variants thought to be of indigenous make, and are joined by a trio of large radomes not before seen. Additionally, updated versions of the Soviet Nikhrom-RRM identification friend or foe (IFF) system fill out the front mast, while a number of conspicuous systems (six smaller and two larger) arranged loosely around the masts are believed to

be part of an electronic warfare system of unknown design. Their appearance is reminiscent of the Japanese NOLQ-3 or Russian RK-25 series electronic warfare suite and associated electronic support measures (ESM) antennas.[12] While reports of Russian electronic warfare systems surfaced concurrently with the launch, state media suggested the ship's electronic warfare, radar and fire-control suites were the fruit of an indigenous development drive, with the latter in particular being enabled by advances in AI technology.[13] Although the recently introduced copy of the Type 362 search radar makes a recurrence, the once ubiquitous MR-104 Drum Tilt fire-control radars have been replaced by a pair of small phased array radars. Likewise, two EO devices of a bulkier design than hitherto seen have been fitted to the masts for optical surveillance. Aside from mere surveillance and targeting, the ship's highly prominent bridge and other superstructures suggest it is configured for a central role in C4I (command, control, communications, computers and intelligence) as well. For detection beneath the waves, a sonar system is fitted to the bow. On the hull itself, the addition of bilge keels and active stabilisers emphasise the size of the vessel and showcases serious consideration went into ensuring performance in choppy waters. The ship's propulsion system is of an unknown type, as are the actual engines that power it: it is possible that the single Russian Krivak III-class frigate transferred in the early 2000s may be put to good use after all, by donating (part of) its combined gas turbine and gas turbine (COGAG) propulsion system. However, given that the ship was transferred as scrap and only one of its smaller cruise gas turbines was ever displayed a decade and a half after it was dismantled, it is uncertain whether all four turbines are even available – with the prospect of other large naval vessels joining the fleet essentially ruling out this possibility. The newfound open amity

The Nampho frigate in March 2025. Note the long bilge keels and cut-outs (obscured by the scaffolding) where active stabilisers are to be fitted. (KCBC)

Kim Jong Un and the crew complement of the *Choe Hyon* pose proudly in front of their new ship during its launch ceremony in Nampho, May 2025. (KCBC)

Kim Jong Un inspects one of the Krivak III-class's DO-63 cruise gas turbines at the Pukjung naval factory in 2023. North Korea's ambitions to build larger naval vessels will necessitate investments in a multitude of new technologies, including marine propulsion and shipborne radars. (KCBC)

between Russia and the DPRK may also provide outcome, although if recent rhetoric about its naval ambitions is to be believed, aid in setting up an indigenous turbine industry is more likely. For the moment, it is unclear whether engines are even fitted, with the propulsion system possibly absent during weapons tests in April 2025.[14] Moreover, statements made by Kim Jong Un later suggested new ship propulsion technologies were still under development.[15] Satellite images taken of Nampho in September 2025 might indicate that engine installation was underway at this date.[16]

Despite already surpassing all naval ship construction efforts previously undertaken, no time was wasted before expanding the scope of the project. A second ship in the new class to lead the east coast fleet was under construction starting already in October 2024, with assembly progressing at similarly impressive speeds.[17] A mere month after the launch of the lead ship, the second was deemed ready for its own maritime initiation (albeit without any weapons or subsystems installed). However, whereas the Nampho facilities featured a floating drydock capable of safely setting the ship afloat, the Chongjin facilities are more limited, and necessitated a much more dramatic sideways launch from a slipway ashore. A lack of recent experience with such launches spelled disaster however, and in a widely publicised incident the ship was damaged during the procedure. The rear of the ship apparently began its movement

prematurely, causing the ship to topple over and parts of the hull to be damaged in the process. Recovery efforts were extensive and righting the ship ultimately took just two weeks, after which the ship was towed to Rajin for repairs and finalisation of its construction. Evidently, the setback has not diminished the North Korean appetite for naval upheaval, and ambitious timelines were set for its restoration. Already on 12 June, a launch ceremony was held in Rajin, albeit achieved only by cutting some clear corners in order to get the ship externally presentable. Various systems including the four NLOS launchers had yet to be installed, and no shots of the interior of either destroyer have been shown, leaving the possibility that significant work remains to be done before commissioning.[18] Nevertheless, no damage to the second ship, named the *Kang Kon*, were apparent, and only insubstantial differences in its construction compared to the lead ship can be discerned.

Banners at the Nampho build site meanwhile seemed to suggest an intended commission date of January 2026, which would be unprecedented considering the project's scope and complexity of its subsystems.[19] An August inspection of the lead ship showed that outfitting of the interior was progressing rapidly, with the crew quarters, bridge, and command centre seemingly finished. Nevertheless, shots of the latter two were later determined to have been photoshopped. Work on the exterior was meanwhile still ongoing, and the large phased array radars, AK-630 copies and NLOS launchers were conspicuously missing, while one of the decoy launchers had been moved to a different location.[20] The result of these changes became apparent during another inspection in early October, during which substantial changes to the ship's subsystems were revealed. The front VLS now features 24 cells in total, seemingly exchanging the tentative Pyoljji-3 cells for more Pyoljji-1-sized cells. While the middle VLS section was left unchanged, the suspected ballistic missile cells farther to the aft were replaced by a much wider segment thought to contain another 24 Pyoljji-1-sized cells. It remains unknown whether these cells are compatible with Hwasal-series cruise missiles as well, in which case the move towards a greater degree of standardisation would make sense. Despite the omission of ballistic missiles, commentary by Kim Jong Un affirmed that the ship remained destined to be nuclear-armed.[21] Other changes to the aft are uncertain, but the widening of the VLS section likely means the UAV hangars have been removed. Likewise, the NLOS launchers are no longer fitted. CIWS capabilities gained a surprise boost however, with the two AK-630 copies now replaced by an entirely new CIWS

The destroyer *Kang Kon* during its (re)launch ceremony at a dry dock in Rajin in June 2025. Note that the NLOS launchers normally present next to the exhaust stack are not yet fitted. (KCBC)

design resembling the Dutch Goalkeeper or the Chinese Type 730. While employing a more modern layout incorporating an integrated fire-control radar and EO device, Soviet inheritance remains visible in its AK-630-derived sextuple barrel. The radar suite was also remodelled, with the small phased array radars proven mock-ups by their replacement by a new design reminiscent of the Chinese Type 347 (as well as a North Korean design only exported to Myanmar). Given that the new CIWS has its own integrated fire-control radar of a different design, a greater degree of redundancy was thus introduced. New mast structures furthermore improve crew access to the radar systems, and the ship's bridge, combat information centre (CIC) and crew quarters now genuinely appear to have been furnished. While the ship is destined to enter service in the near future, these radical last-minute changes underline how much its design is still being figured out even as it is built, and it is likely that other ships in the class will be subject to similarly capricious changes. Moreover, with seemingly completed systems repeatedly proven to be temporary mock-ups instead, there is no way of verifying when any vessel has actually attained operation status.

Meanwhile, state media commentary suggests more destroyers in the class as well as support vessels and even a cruiser are being planned, with two ships of equal size or greater than the Choe Hyon-class annually being the stated aim (next year's examples evidently also being of the Choe Hyon-class).[22, 23] Such bold claims may be backed up sooner rather than later, with construction work on new naval craft apparently having already commenced at both Chongjin and Nampho as of May 2025.[24] A July inspection of the build site in Nampho unveiled that it concerned the third Choe Hyon-class, and that construction is slated to be finished by the 10th of October 2026.[25]

By linking up its land-based assets with ocean-going platforms North Korea could begin to project force over far greater distances than the hermit kingdom has historically been known to. In fact, if the DPRK was looking to assert itself more boldly the new destroyers could become the first military ships (since the captured USS *Pueblo* in 1999) to move between the North's two isolated coasts. The fact that both destroyers produced thus far have been assigned to the West Sea Fleet suggests that such a transit is all but certain in the near future. Moreover, North Korea could soon start to link up with foreign allies such as Russia and Iran for joint exercises or even limited combat operations. Such movements could set the stage for new propaganda coups for the North, and drastically alter the nature of potential confrontations between it and its adversaries. And indeed, Kim Jong Un's reported statement during the *Kang Kon*'s launch ceremony that 'the enemies will soon experience how offending and unpleasant it is to have to watch their rival's warships run rampant on the fringes of their territorial waters' leaves little doubt about a more assertive role for the KPAN in the future. While grandiose plans are nothing out of the ordinary for the North, there can be little doubt that this sudden surge in shipbuilding success is enabled at least partly by technical or even material assistance from Russia. The consequences of these nations bundling their capabilities are not to be underestimated: if the current trend continues the KPAN is set to transform to a far greater degree in the next decade than it has in the previous five.

Modernisation efforts are not entirely limited to the introduction of new naval vessels however. Aside from the refitting of many older craft with the now ubiquitous 14.5mm rotary machine gun weapon stations, one particular class has been deemed worthy of a

The destroyer *Choe Hyon* displays its new CIWS, radar suite and reworked masts during an inspection in October of 2025. (KCBC)

The interior of the bridge of the destroyer *Choe Hyon*. A surprisingly high degree of digitisation is apparent, including what appears to be a large Electronic Chart System (ECS) to aid in navigation. (KCBC)

The combat information center (CIC) of the destroyer *Choe Hyon*. Earlier images which showed a radically different, much less digitised, layout were believed to be photoshopped. (KCBC)

The destroyer *Choe Hyon* moored in Nampho after weapons tests in April 2025. Barely visible at left, the by comparison underwhelming products of the 2010s: the Amnok and Tuman-class corvettes, and modernised Najin-class frigate. (KCBC)

complete overhaul: the KPAN's pride of old, the Najin-class. These ships, both of which already underwent an extensive redesign in the 1980s to bring their weaponry up to the standards of North Korean technology of the time, have not stood the passing of time well and in their original configuration had become close to useless. Rather than indefinitely postponing their retirement beyond obsolescence like other KPAN vessels or scrapping them like the Soho-class, at the start of 2013 work began to rebuild the craft and incorporate the new weaponry that has become available. By mid 2014, the refit had been finished, and the full extent of changes made became apparent. To save resources, much of the weapons systems that were previously present have been left untouched, including the two 100mm cannons, forward dual 57mms, six dual 25mm weapon stations, the MR-104 Drum Tilt radar and much of the general layout of the ship. However, its characteristic P-15 type AShMs were removed, and in their place two racks for a total of eight Kumsong-3 launch tubes were fitted with room to spare. Other changes included the removal of the aft dual 57mm station, in the place of which the two legacy AK-230 CIWS were placed side-by-side. Where the aft AK-230 had stood a MANPADS-based SAM station has been fitted, and beside it another six 82mm smoke/chaff launchers were installed. Another addition to the ship's already cramped rear deck are two double 533mm torpedo launchers fitted extremely closely around the 100mm turret. Minor alterations in its radar suite are also apparent; its air search radar was removed and a Furuno-type radar installed instead, and attached to the rear funnel is now a covered dome presumably housing an aiming station. The upgrades provide the class with some much-needed enhanced weaponry, but they fall far short of bringing it to

A close-up of the Amnok and Tuman-class corvettes, and modernised Najin-class frigate at Nampho in April 2025. Note that the Amnok-class's AShMs are not fitted. (KCBC)

terms with the modern age, and as it stands the capabilities of the Najin remain akin more to a small FAC than a frigate, albeit with a lot more gun-based firepower. What is more, only one of the two Najin-class ships has been overhauled, and although the other has returned to its construction port of Rajin since mid 2016, there is no indication that it will receive similar treatment. Instead, its continued presence at this location could indicate that after half a century of service this vessel is finally heading towards retirement.

7

GUNBOATS AND MISSILE BOATS

Development of new generations of warships began to take-off in earnest by the late 2000s, and a range of other projects aimed at both upgrading existing classes with modern equipment as well as introducing novel classes were slowly taking form. The first project to incorporate new weapons systems onto smaller conventional naval vessels aimed to introduce a range of new 40 to 46-metre gunboats and missile boats to the KPAN. Their precise number is difficult to ascertain due to the fact that their production is distributed amongst many different ports and harbours, as well as the relatively small size of the craft involved. Additionally, the diversity of classes in this displacement range means that virtually all craft differ from one another in some way or another, suggesting that the North Koreans are encountering difficulties with standardising production.

The construction of the first of these gunboats began in the early 2010s in Nampho, with the hull laid down at the northern port of Yongampo, traditionally a hovercraft factory, and although the hull, weaponry and radar suite were quickly fitted, a lengthy docking at Nampho lasting until 2016 suggests difficulties were encountered during some part of its construction or trials. At least two successors in the same class were laid down immediately after the first hull was completed, and two craft in this class are now confirmed to have entered service at Sagot naval base near the NLL. Fitted with much of the weaponry found on both the cutting edge in North Korean shipbuilding as well as gunboats dating from the 1960s, its

main armament is composed of either a turreted 85mm or 100mm cannon on the bow, depending on the ship, supported by a 30mm CIWS based on the AK-630 and a SAM station that can be fitted with six MANPADS aft, as well as what appears to be a dual 37mm cannon station. Two 14.5mm rotary machine gun stations straddle an MR-104 Drum Tilt radar used to direct the 30mm CIWS aft of the bridge. The radar mast appears to inherit many of the radars also seen on the SES series of craft. The 30mm has aiming stations to allow for manual targeting of ships or slow-flying aircraft when radars have become jammed or damaged, located on the fore and aft of the raised bridge structure.

On the west coast, two examples of another class measuring 43 metres were laid down in Nampho in 2013, but have seemingly undergone weapons fitting in a different harbour since, making analysis of its precise capabilities difficult beyond the fact that it does not appear to use the 76mm OTO Melara either. Tracking of the new patrol ship construction programme has been similarly difficult on the east coast, where a 46-metre long vessel was spotted at Sinpho harbour in late 2015 before being deployed to Rakwon. Although its CIWS and radar suite are limited, comprising one 30mm AK-630 copy but no fire-control radars, this vessel is the first in KPAN service confirmed to be armed with a new 10-barrelled anti-submarine rocket launcher. Although closely resembling the 213mm RBU-6000, the calibre is instead thought to match the 252mm RBU-1200 found on many KPAN vessels for logistics reasons. Given the RBU-1200 rocket's extremely limited range, the possibility that another calibre has been substituted cannot be ruled out however. Despite mimicking a system from the early 1960s, the system represents an improvement over the five-barrelled RBU-1200, which has to be manually reloaded and can only be targeted by steering the entire ship. Reloading of the RBU-6000 is automated, with the loading system feeding individual rounds into the launcher from a magazine located below deck; it remains unknown whether such functionality has been replicated. While details regarding sonar are lacking, the lack of any other anti-submarine warfare weaponry indicates that the vessel essentially constitutes a very limited anti-submarine warfare platform. A smaller offshoot of this design is under production on the west coast, with three vessels observed under construction at Nampho in early 2024. What is powering these ships (and many other new North Korean naval projects) is uncertain, but it is possible that Soviet-legacy marine diesel engines like the M503 have been replaced by imports, such as an MTU 16V 396 TE74L spotted at the Munchon naval factory in 2016. Alternatively, there is some indication of indigenous development of such diesel engines, with models displayed at the Pukjung naval factory in 2023 that appear to have been based on the MAN D2842 and MTU 12V 2000 series.

Back on the eastern seaboard, a 32-metre long missile boat was launched in late 2016, although its public debut came only in 2023. Its armament suite is remarkable for this size class in the DPRK. Two dual Kumsong-3 launchers fitted behind the bridge provide an anti-ship capability which has so far been reserved for new experimental craft like the SES or other larger naval vessels. Since smaller craft typically lack the radars to fully exploit the range of AShMs, the vessel must rely on proper C4ISR systems to ensure a target can be acquired through other means. Though the proliferation of capable AShMs on smaller platforms is of concern, perhaps an even more notable introduction on this vessel is a new variant of the 76mm OTO Melara copy, which has been housed in a compact and lightweight cupola reminiscent of the 76/62 Sovraponte. Like the Sovraponte, it was likely designed to offer the performance of a rapid-firing 76mm cannon in a smaller turret that does not penetrate the ship's deck. Unlike the Sovraponte, an integrated guidance system does not appear to be available. The sleek gun mount features two of the North's NLOS missiles installed in canisters on either side, essentially merging a potent gun system with a limited anti-ship missile capability into a single weapons system. The successful integration of this gun system may signal the start of a wider introduction of such lightweight 76mm mounts to smaller KPAN naval vessels. Nevertheless, no fire-control radar is present, and this vessel is the first larger KPAN design in two decades to omit the installation of an AK-630 copy, although it does feature a SAM station with six MANPADS positioned to the aft. With only one vessel of this class produced in over half a decade thus far, it is too early to ascertain whether North Korea believes this vessel merits production in any meaningful numbers. However, a trend toward vessels prioritising ease of production over advanced technologies in hull design and propulsion is evident. Widespread introduction of such vessels could be a severe nuisance, especially to larger ROKN ships, as they have a small profile themselves while boasting impressive anti-ship capabilities when swarming. In this regard they could be considered the modern equivalent of the Soviet-legacy Komar-class, which was of comparably small stature but can still claim the first sinking by AShMs of the Israeli destroyer INS *Eilat* shortly after the Six-Day War in 1967.

Three patrol or missile boats under construction at Nampho in early 2024. Completion of these vessels may still take considerable time, as the outfitting process for even smaller crafts can extend over many years in North Korea. (KCBC)

The 32-metre-long missile boat seen with the submarine *Hero Kim Gun-Ok* in the background just before its launch at Sinpo in late 2023. (KCBC)

While the copy of the 76mm OTO Melara rapid-fire cannon is ideally suited for short-ranged naval engagements, North Korea instead opted for a turreted 85mm (pictured) or 100mm cannon as the main armament of the new class of 40m gunboats. Secondary armament includes a 30mm AK-630 copy slaved to an MR-104 Drum Tilt radar, two 14.5mm rotary machine guns, what is believed to be a dual 37mm cannon with a protective canopy and a SAM station, all but the latter with a dual purpose function against both sea and air targets. As this artwork is based on currently available (satellite) imagery, loadout and details might differ from what can be seen here. (Artwork by Anderson Subtil)

While the SES series of craft incorporate advanced technologies in hull design and propulsion, vessels of roughly similar length like this 46-metre long patrol boat are significantly cheaper to produce due to their more conventional construction, providing the KPAN with a more cost-efficient alternative. Nevertheless, production of this class has been limited to a single ship on the east coast. The primary role of this vessel is anti-submarine warfare, for which purposes it sports a single 10-tube anti-submarine rocket launcher, yet curiously lacking any other anti-submarine warfare weaponry. Other armament is typical for new KPAN vessels, comprising an AK-630 copy, a MANPADS-based SAM station and two 14.5mm rotary machine guns located in front of the bridge. As this artwork is based on currently available imagery, the hull below the waterline might differ from what can be seen here. (Artwork by Anderson Subtil)

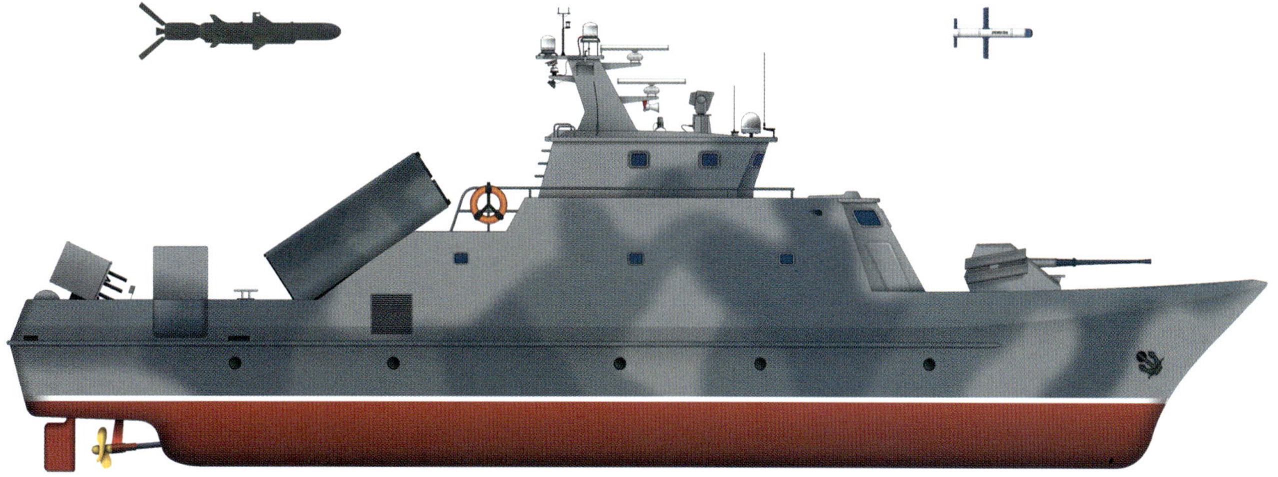

The 32-metre long missile boat/FAC represents one of the newest inventions of North Korea's naval industry. The relatively uncomplicated design seems well-suited for mass production, though it remains uncertain whether North Korea has plans to that effect. Though innovation in hull design or propulsion may be lacking, the vessel's armament suite serves as a redeeming factor, featuring a newly developed compact and lightweight 76mm gun mount coupled with four of the North's NLOS missiles that can be employed against both small naval vessels and ground targets. Long-range armament consists of four Kumsong-3 AShMs positioned aft of the bridge, accompanied by a SAM station based on MANPADS. Notably, there is no CIWS present. (Artwork by Anderson Subtil)

Fast Attack Craft

The introduction of a new generation of warships to the KPAN may have resulted in a shift of tactics corresponding to the weaponry that has become available, but the overall doctrine remains mostly unchanged. Since this has in the past included the use of vast numbers of FAC and torpedo boats, ongoing development of craft in these classes is not unexpected. Having produced hundreds of FAC based on already proven designs until the mid 1980s, North Korea has now begun designing a variety of new types of entirely indigenous origin. For this it leans on experience gained during the production efforts of the previous century, but also through designing several types of infiltration vessels, combining their low observability and evasive capabilities with the offensive capabilities of true torpedo boats. However, despite the fact that the KPAN is ripe for such new designs, these types have primarily been built for export, and few if any have entered operational service in North Korea. While heavily marketed to foreign customers by front companies such as Kay Marine Sdn Bhd and the Green Pine Associated Corporation, the naval arm of Iran's Revolutionary Guard so far appears to have been the sole customer. It imported all classes so far known to have been designed in 2002 and has subsequently produced large numbers of their own, several of which were subsequently exported to Syria. Although there is as yet no indication that these craft will also be produced in numbers for the KPAN, with only those used in promotional videos still berthed in Pyongyang and Wonsan, their interesting design and the technologies they utilise warrant a detailed analysis. Mainly configured for the type of coastal operations North Korea is wont to execute, they feature low, wave-piercing hulls, radar reflecting shapes and internally stored weaponry which is only extruded upon firing. These factors allow them a very high top speed and improved capabilities in adverse weather conditions, in exchange for sacrifices in their offensive and defensive weaponry. Rather than standing their ground, these boats rely on their speed, stealth characteristics and evasive capabilities to avoid and break away from enemy contact.

The smallest and simplest design comes in the form of a 16-metre long craft (US DoD designation Taedong C) with an enclosed bridge that is flush with the hull. Its armament is very light, consisting of just two 324mm torpedo tubes in compartments concealed in the hull. These torpedoes are of an indigenous North Korean design that likely has its roots in the Chinese Yu-7 ASW torpedo or the Italian A-244S (which could have been acquired from Libya). By design it is very lightweight, and as such mostly limited to use against submarines and small surface combatants.[1] Although it is uncertain whether it can still be employed in the former role, ASW variants of this 324mm torpedo could be quite potent especially when deployed from small submarines. Against surface combatants it would be much less effective, despite employing advanced seeker methods such as passive acoustic and wake-homing. A single retractable Furuno radar dome forms the boat's radar suite, which is sufficient given its armament's short range – its shortcomings mitigated by the craft's very high speed of up to 52 knots. This craft was marketed abroad as the TB 16 (Torpedo Boat, 16 metres) and purchased by Iran where it is known as the IPS-16/Peykaap, and has spawned a family of closely related craft. Some of these are outfitted with AShMs and upgraded radar masts, but thereby forgo much of the stealth gained by the sleek features of the original configuration. Names associated with these variants include Peykaap II/III, Zolfaghar and Bavar, with four of the craft exported to Venezuela in 2023. A related North Korean naval craft exported as the TB 16D is for a large part identical in its design, but incorporates the unique ability to submerge itself almost entirely in the water, leaving only its cabin exposed to potential

The doors of the TB 16(D)'s concealed torpedo compartment are only opened just before launching the torpedo so as to reduce the craft's radar cross-section. (Authors' archive)

A TB 16D running semi-submerged. Both the TB 16 and TB 16D were marketed to foreign customers via flashy marketing videos and front companies located abroad. (Authors' archive)

observers in exchange for a lower top speed of some 40 knots while fully surfaced. This craft has also been exported to Iran, where it is known as the Gahjae.

A craft exported as the TB 17D takes this concept even further, using a design which is rooted much more in the various submersible fast infiltration craft developed for the intelligence agencies over the years than in the new generation of FACs. Armed with two 324mm torpedo tubes, it can travel completely submerged like a submarine, in so doing outperforming the TB 16D and early-generation submersible fast infiltration craft which had to stay still while submerged or move as a semi-submersible. For this purpose it features a sleek, highly streamlined hull 17-metres in length with retractable radar and optics and no windows. Three different types of propulsion provide varying degrees of mobility while surfaced; in semi-submersible mode, using a snorkel to provide air for the engine; and fully submerged using electrical thrusters. Although its export designation hints at a continued role as a torpedo boat, these characteristics also make it ideally suited for short-ranged infiltration missions, and by extension a career in the RGB or even SOF would serve it well. To extend its range on such missions, the TB 17D can be fitted with conformal fuel tanks mounted on the upper surface of the hull, increasing its operational range while seemingly preserving its torpedo-carrying capacity. These add-on sections also feature hatches for diver access. At least two TB 17Ds were delivered to Iran in 2002 alongside other FAC, which renamed the craft initially as the Kajami-class, and more recently the Zulfikar-class (US DoD designation Taedong B).

A TB 17D takes to the surface after running fully submerged much like a submarine. (Authors' archive)

Never accepted into KPAN service, the single prototype of the PB 21 survives to this day berthed in a corner of one of Wonsan's shipyards. Note the boxes for the huge 533mm torpedoes sticking out of the otherwise streamlined hull. (Authors' archive)

A larger torpedo boat carrying far more powerful 533mm torpedoes was also developed, and is known as the PB 21 (Patrol Boat, 21 metres) on the export market. Similarly slick in its design as the TB 16D, its two torpedo tubes are embedded in stealthily angled boxes running from the stern to the front of the cabin, the only other armament being a pintle mount for a 12.7mm DShK mounted to the aft, which appears to be an Iranian addition. New torpedoes have also been developed since the introduction of torpedo boats, with tubes of the same diameter as in the previous century incorporating new technologies such as acoustic/wake-homing. Examples of these include the YT-534W1 (presumably 534mm in diameter as opposed to 533mm) and CHT-02D, the latter of which was also supposedly responsible for the 2010 sinking of the *Cheonan*. New torpedoes do much to enhance the capabilities and EW-resistance of torpedo boats, but since they can also be used by older types carrying the same tubes they are not a unique feature of the PB 21. The radar suite of the craft is identical to that of the TB 16, and its top speed is also believed to be some 52 knots. In Iran, this craft is known as the IPS-18 Tir, a redesigned variant of which is known as the Tir II-class. This craft is equipped with AShMs and a much larger radar mast, and was in turn exported to Syria.

With the advent of widespread drone adoption in the KPA, the country's naval industry has also begun experimentation on unmanned designs. Any details of such unmanned (semi-) submersible vessels remain highly obscure, with one type unveiled as a model during the 'Military Hardware Exhibition Defence Development-2025'. Due to a lack of suitable imagery for analysis, its size, specifications, and role can only be guessed at, with infiltration, reconnaissance, sabotage and even the possibility of being armed with torpedoes all belonging to the realm of possibilities. It may be assumed that the craft builds on earlier experience building small unmanned craft, combining elements of the TB 17D with technologies such as new EO devices, advances in AI, and inertial guidance methods.

Very Slender Vessels

Few if any of these vessels entered service with the KPAN, presumably because their capabilities were judged below the level required to warrant large production to replace or at least supplement older FAC in North Korean service, despite being relatively easily mass-produced. Nevertheless, there is some indication that development of these FAC has continued, and the future production of replacement craft for the legacy fleet of torpedo boats cannot be ruled out. In the meantime, another family of ships would provide a far more advanced FAC role in the DPRK, leaning on a different technology for its effectiveness. Due to their extremely sleek and peculiarly shaped hull, these vessels are generally identified as VSVs, which combine stealth characteristics with the very high speed of the aforementioned FAC with heavier armament. Its unique shape means that these ships are capable of piercing waves rather than mounting them, therefore allowing them to reach much greater speeds than regular FAC while maintaining stability. In the DPRK, the VSV family spans several designs up to roughly 34 metres in length, and can be divided into at least seven types with several subvariants each, collectively known as the Nalchi-class by the US DoD. Spanning both coasts and spawning well over a dozen warships, the programme's size is the likely cause for the many different variants that exist, making it difficult to pin down the exact capabilities and specifications of the entire VSV force currently entering service.

By virtue of incorporating the most emergent technologies, the smaller VSVs arguably represent the most innovative part of the programme. These autonomous surface vessels with a length of less than 10 metres, first spotted during a March 2013 inspection by Kim Jong Un of the Pyongyang factory where they are built, combine remote operating capabilities with low observability and an electro-optical device for observation and targeting. Designed for use along preprogrammed routes in coastal areas, they incorporate advances in radio/communications technologies into the VSV hull which is powered by a simple outboard motor. They lack any armament or explosive payload, and the fact that they are of small size means their range and operations will be relatively limited. Nevertheless, the introduction of unmanned surface vessels (USVs) to the KPAN is a remarkable feat, telling of modern North Korean investments in communications and electronics, contrasting starkly with the common image associated with the North's navy. Such investments also aim to bring in revenue from abroad, and the North Korean Glocom front company markets for export a telemetry/control system for unmanned aerial vehicles (UAVs) and USVs under the designation GS-2600-01, which supposedly works out to a range of over 100 kilometres for a duration of up to four hours under ECM conditions.[2] Given the small size of the vessels to which it would be fitted and their mission scope, this should be sufficient for most situations.

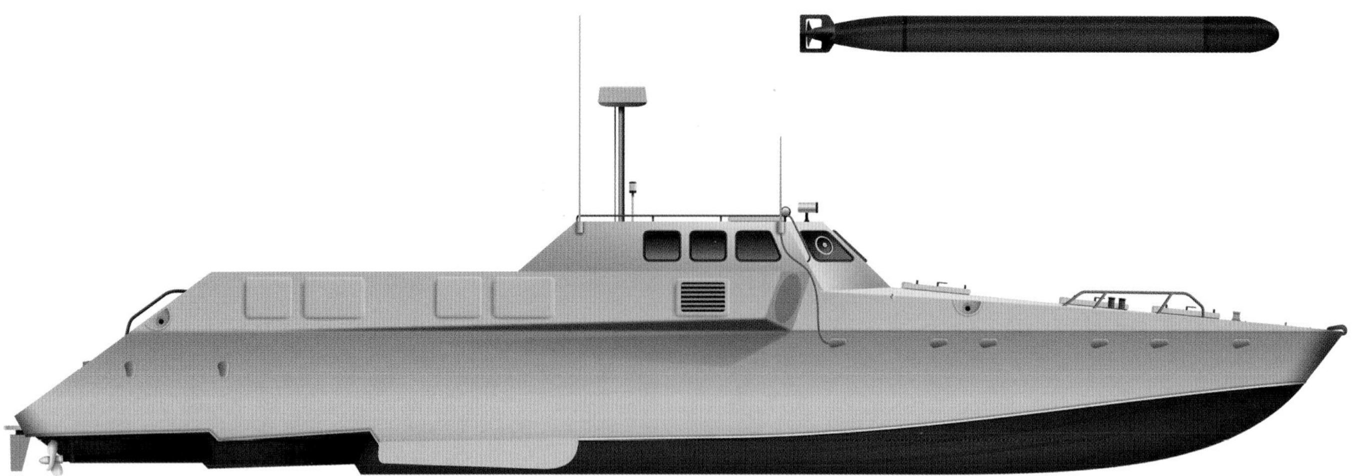

Compared to the smaller TB 16, the PB 21 carries far more powerful 533mm torpedoes housed in stealthily angled boxes running from the stern until the front of the cabin. The change in armament necessitated an increase in length to some 21 metres, as an apparent result of which the craft received the patrol boat (PB) designation. Apart from room for a pintle-mounted machine gun no other secondary (gun) armament is present, making the design particularly vulnerable to enemy ships and aircraft alike. However, as with all other KPAN ships, crew-served MANPADS can partly compensate for a lack of air defences. (Artwork by Anderson Subtil)

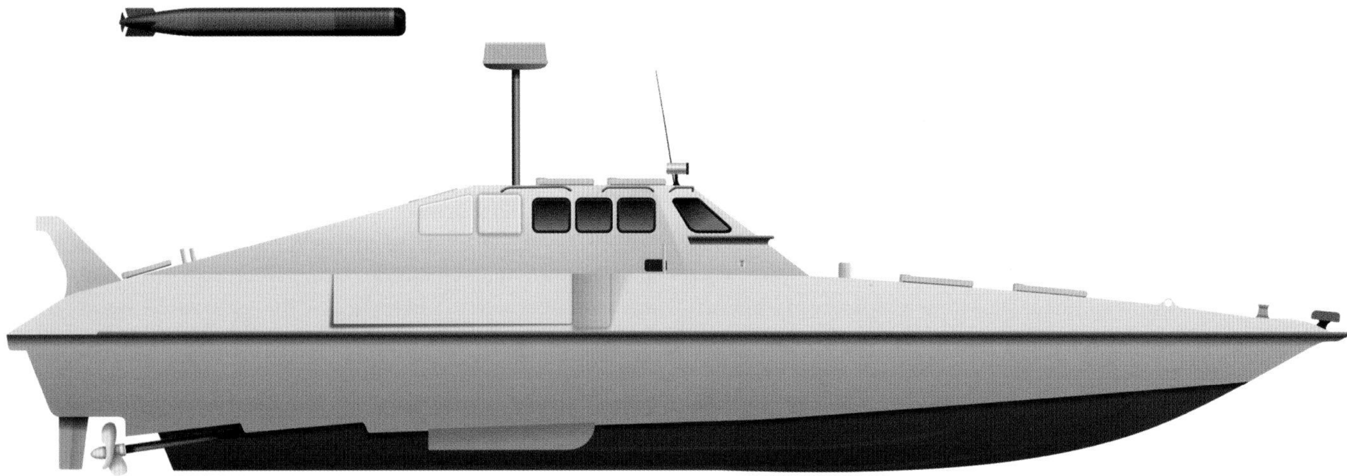

It seems likely that even the TB 16D's high speed and ability to submerge itself almost entirely did not redeem the craft's underwhelming loadout of two concealed short-ranged 324mm torpedoes and no defensive armament. The craft's ability to partly submerge may aid it in remaining undetected for longer, but along the nowadays carefully monitored (by both optical and radar equipment) coasts of South Korea it may no longer be sufficient. Perhaps unsurprisingly, despite the relatively low construction costs the KPAN apparently did not warrant the TB 16(D)'s combat capabilities as sufficient to replace its vast fleet of 1950s era fast attack craft. (Artwork by Anderson Subtil)

The TB 17D is a progressive development of the submersible fast infiltration craft developed for North Korea's foreign intelligence agencies. The TB 17D combines two 324mm torpedo tubes with the unique capability to move at very high speeds while surfaced, as a semi-submersible (using a snorkel to provide air for the engine) or fully submerged (using electrical thrusters) like a submarine. Although these characteristics make it ideally suited for laying underwater ambushes against enemy combatants along the Korean coasts, the TB 17D does not appear to have entered service (in any significant numbers) in North Korea. (Artwork by Anderson Subtil)

Kim Jong Un inspects the USV design during a March 2013 visit to the December 7 Factory (Unit 1501) in Pyongyang. In the back, another 29-metre long (manned) VSV. (KCBC)

Of course, larger VSVs are operated by a sizeable crew. Still, the electronics incorporated in their command structure remain a vast improvement over the previous generation of warships still in use with the KPAN, a fact which has been specifically emphasised in their scarce media coverage. Measuring between 23 and 34 metres, these vessels carry relatively light armament on their slender hull, providing a diverse FAC/patrol ship role ordinarily fulfilled by the KPA's numerous Cold War-legacy P-4 and P-6 derivatives. Since their first sighting in Pyongyang in mid 2012, increasing numbers of VSVs have been spotted on both of the DPRK's coasts, representing perhaps the single greatest introduction of new naval vessels to the KPAN in modern times. The fact that they are small and as a rule swiftly enter service with units where they are stored in underground naval bases, as well as tight security surrounding the project means that many specifics of their construction, capabilities and current number remain a mystery. What imagery is available mostly stems from three visits made by Kim Jong Un in 2012 and 2013 to the Pyongyang factory where they are built. This factory is known as the December 7 Factory when discussing its civilian produce (which includes children's slides as well as maxi pads) but also as Unit 1501 in reference to its military applications, which have in the past included the manufacture of midget submarines, drones and technology demonstrators for various

kinds of naval craft. Although the first VSVs were all spotted here, production later expanded to Nampho and Ryongampho on the west coast, and Chongjin and Wonsan on the east coast.

The oldest and smallest VSVs measure roughly 23 metres in length and have a stealthy, angular appearance. Their radar-reducing features are broken only by a manually-aimed SAM station on the stern which can be fitted with two MANPADS, as well as a small radar mast on the bridge. Offensive capabilities are boosted by torpedoes in concealed compartments, which are either of the new 324mm type or, more likely, 553mm torpedoes. Production of these craft has been especially prolific on the west coast, but their introduction has also begun in south-eastern naval bases, with a total of over nine craft as of yet produced. Their larger brethren, measuring some 29 metres, trade some of their stealth and ease of production for an expansion of their armament suite. Their stealthy lines, which ensure the bridge is flush with the hull, are maintained, but a larger aft deck accommodates two automated 4x6 107mm MRLs as well as two of the dual MANPADS stations, with a third 4x6 107mm MRL located just in front of the radar mast atop the bridge. Two 533mm torpedo tubes are ingeniously fitted through the hull alongside the bridge, with their rears exposed on the aft deck. This armament is further supported by what appears to be a 30mm AK-630 installed on the bow. These larger craft have enjoyed a slightly smaller production run, but nevertheless entered service at a quick rate at both coasts' more southern naval bases – the fact that they are typically stationed in underground naval bases there means their number is difficult to estimate. The third and largest manned VSV variant is considerably more labour and resource intensive to construct, with a total of over half-a-dozen currently slowly entering service after production commenced in Nampho in 2013 and shortly thereafter in Chongjin. These vessels are characterised by the same general layout as their smaller sister ships, but notably break some of their stealthily sleek surfaces by the inclusion of an indigenous 30mm CIWS based on the AK-630 on the bow, and a bridge which is no longer flush with the hull due to two walkways which straddle it on either side. A tall radar mast sits atop it that bears a modest radar suite and the same EO device installed on other modern naval vessels like the Amnok-class. At roughly 34 metres in length, they feature a large raised aft deck which is sheltered by raised walls on either side, housing the ship's main armament made up of two conspicuous launchers

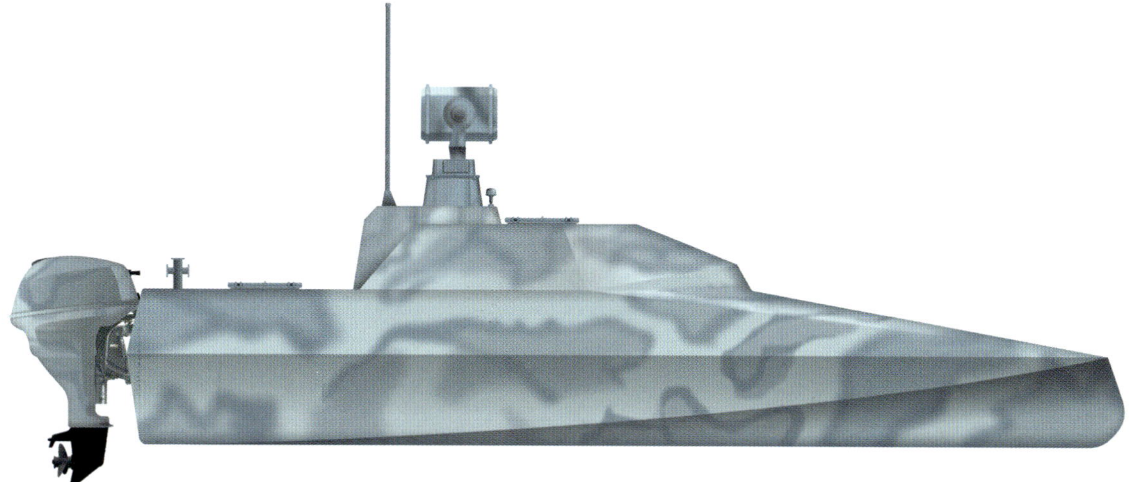

The smaller VSV design is optimised for surveillance and targeting missions along the Korean coast. Featuring a wave-piercing hull whose sides slope inward, the design introduces two novel features to the KPAN: remote operating capabilities and an EO device. A simple outboard motor powers the craft, which although certainly less novel than some of its other features is sufficient for operations following preprogrammed routes in coastal areas. Although North Korea's interest in this development remains uncertain, such craft naturally lend themselves to carrying an explosive payload and engaging enemy vessels by ramming into them. As this artwork is based on currently available imagery, the front section might differ from what can be seen here. (Artwork by Anderson Subtil)

on the stern of the vessel. Like the 29-metre VSV, the hull contains compartments for two 533mm torpedoes, further completing the ship's weapon suite. Detailed imagery to confirm the contents of the two launchers on the stern is lacking, but one possibility is that they contain quadruple mounts for North Korea's new NLOS missile. This missile is being introduced on various ground-based platforms, but is also known to use a naval launcher which has been seen fitted during testing on a gunboat. If it is indeed this system, it provides these VSVs with an interesting striking capability against land and small naval targets, with a range that could be up to 40 kilometres judging by its similarity to the Chinese CM-501GA. Whatever the case, the armament in question might well be the most advanced feature of this craft, and consequently also the reason why none of them have seemingly entered active service.

Contrary to other new vessels under construction in the DPRK, the VSVs are produced at a relatively quick pace, likely owing to their small size and the fact that none of the ships appear to carry complicated missile or radar technology. Most have since entered service quickly (with the notable exception of the 34-metre long examples), mainly with southern naval bases such Sagot and Changjon. Should production continue, a respectable fleet of VSVs could be in active service by the end of the 2020s, a fact which will have to be taken into consideration for wartime planning. Unconfirmed reports state Kim Jong Un had ordered the mass production of the VSVs during a visit to the Chongjin shipyard in July 2018, suggesting this is indeed the North Koreans' intention.[3] Such a fleet would be ideal for harassing

ROKN ships, patrolling the DPRK's maritime borders and assisting transport craft in blitz landings in the early stages of a war, using their MRLs to soften coastal defences in advance. In the meantime, new variants of varying sizes incorporating other emerging technologies are certain to see the light of day, with a potential infiltration variant with a length of 16 metres laid up at the December 7 Factory since 2016. However, the early to mid 2020s brought no indication of an acceleration of their construction programmes, and aside from about half-a-dozen 34-metre long examples still being worked on the programme appears largely dormant.

A menacing sight: the 30mm AK-630 copy on a 34-metre VSV seen during a visit by Kim Jong Un to the Chongjin shipyard in July 2018. (KCBC)

The rear deck of the 29-metre VSV showing a dual MANPADS station as well as two of the 107mm MRL blocks. (KCBC)

The VSV series distinguishes itself among KPAN naval crafts by incorporating camouflage patterns optimised for operations along Korea's rugged coastlines. Shown is the 34-metre VSV. (KCBC)

The VSVs incorporate modern technology, including multifunction display-equipped control stations, outboard cameras and remote-controlled weaponry. (KCBC)

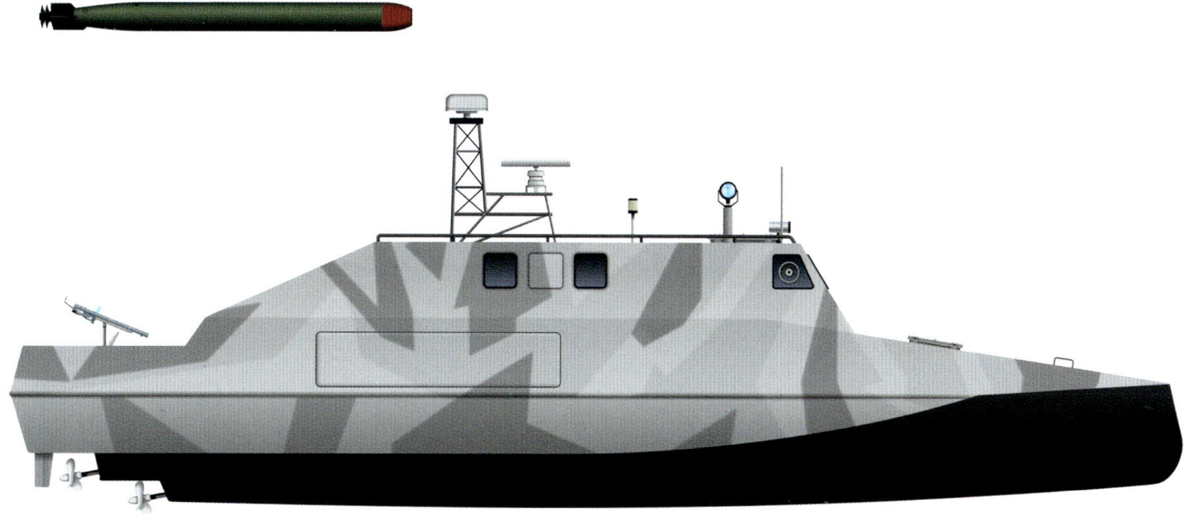

While designing fast attack craft armed with torpedoes as their primary armament in the twenty-first century is already quite unique, producing these as a primary naval vessel in the AShM-rich environment of today is remarkable. The developmental origin of the 23-metre long VSV is a lot less surprising however. Building on design aspects of the PB-21 concept, the 23-metre long VSV further improves on its stealth characteristics while introducing the novel wave-piercing hull concept of the VSV. Although the increase in length has freed up enough space for the installation of a single MANPADS station to cope with aerial threats, the ship still lacks any gun or missile armament, meaning it will have to evade ROKN patrol boats around the coast. As this artwork is based on currently available imagery, the front section might differ from what can be seen here. (Artwork by Anderson Subtil)

Like most other VSVs entering service in recent years, the 29-metre long VSV class sports an attractive camouflage pattern that allows it to blend in with the rocky Korean coastline. As the coastal waters around the peninsula is its destined theatre of operations, the class's armament suite is heavily geared towards short-ranged engagements, for which purpose three blocks of 4x6 107mm MRLs and two 533mm torpedoes fitted through the hull were deemed appropriate. Additionally, a 30mm AK-630 copy fitted to the bow and 2x2 MANPADS stations located on the aft deck provide a basic but capable anti-aircraft defence for a vessel this size. As this artwork is based on currently available imagery, the front section might differ from what can be seen here. (Artwork by Anderson Subtil)

The 34-metre long VSV stands as the largest and, based on its presumed armament, the most capable VSV to be commissioned into the KPAN. Inheriting features from its 29-metre brethren, the 34-metre VSV maintains the loadout of two 533mm torpedoes and an AK-630 copy. However, it substitutes the 107mm MRLs with two unidentifiable launchers positioned at the stern, believed to accommodate quadruple mounts for North Korea's new NLOS missile that has a range of up to 40km. Curiously, there seems to be a lack of a MANPADS station, which means air defence will be reliant on the manually guided AK-630 copy and MANPADS carried by the crew. As this artwork is based on currently available imagery, the hull below the waterline and rear section might differ from what can be seen here. (Artwork by Anderson Subtil)

8

HOVERCRAFT

Ever seeking to exploit the advantages that asymmetrical warfare may bring, North Korea also maintains an uncommonly large military hovercraft fleet – by sheer numbers the largest in the world. Comprised of up to 200, though likely below 150, air-cushioned landing craft of 18.5 and 21 metres long, the fleet has in recent years been the subject of mockery due to exercises in the coverage of which additional craft had been photoshopped to make it appear larger numbers were involved. In spite of the mixed signals this sends about the state of the KPAN's hovercraft fleet, subsequent exercises have affirmed its operational capacity and the fact that the DPRK continues to value its unique capabilities. Designed to land infantry on coastlines otherwise inaccessible to conventional landing craft by moving over the sea rather than through it, North Korea's hovercraft differ from the designs of most countries in their comparatively modest size, lack of dedicated armament (although many hovercraft are fitted for – but not with – a small armed turret) and the inability to transport vehicles or heavy materiel. Although supposedly based on civilian hovercraft technology imported from the United Kingdom and Western Europe in the 1980s, in these aspects they bear a close resemblance to the Soviet Project-1205 Gus-class hovercraft. Whether any direct technology link with any foreign design exists remains unclear however. While certain aspects

match up well with the British Hovercraft Corporation AP1-88, a 1986 attempt to import a second-hand example fell through, and the first reports of a seemingly indigenous hovercraft date back to mid 1987.[1] It is however clear that three types were designed in the late 1980s, the first of which, designated the 'Kong Bang I' by the US DoD, was the largest at 23 metres in length, but never entered serial production; the one prototype still lies on land at North Korea's north-westernmost port of Ryongampo. The Kong Bang II, which measured 21 metres in length but retained the two-propeller propulsion of the Kong Bang I, enjoyed a production run of some 40 examples however, each of which could carry some 50 personnel at a speed of 52 knots. Two distinct subvariants exist, one of which has a much larger space between the cabin and the bow of the craft to create space for an armed turret (which was not ultimately fitted) and likely carries fewer infantry as a result. The last variant, US DoD designation Kong Bang III, is smaller still at some 18.5 metres length, and uses just one propeller, reducing its speed to an estimated 50 knots. In other aspects it is much akin to its larger brothers; fitted for (but not with) a 2x14.5mm turret and carrying 40 infantrymen, it was subject to a much larger production run of some 100 examples.

As with other naval craft, their small size would be a boon to their chances of survival should war erupt, and the fact that

Kong Bang II and Kong Bang III hovercraft during large-scale coastal landing exercises. The vessels shown here could deliver around 600 infantry in one go. (KCBC)

Kong Bang III hovercraft lie ashore near Wonsan. They were displaced here after construction of a new port at their former base commenced in 2015. (Sam Wise)

A deflated Kong Bang III hovercraft. Note the small platforms for MANPADS operators and a single MANPADS just aft of the cockpit. (KCBC)

At some 21 metres length, the Kong Bang II is the largest hovercraft serially produced by North Korea. Over 40 examples each capable of carrying roughly 50 personnel are available to the KPAN to launch amphibious assaults, although such hovercraft will have difficulty penetrating a multi-layered defence due to the advent of modern precision-guided munitions. The type shown here lacks the mount for an armed turret, but can be fitted with two MANPADS for short-range air-defence and is equipped with two Furuno radars for navigation. (Artwork by Anderson Subtil)

hovercraft, as a rule, are quite fast means they may just slip through coastal defences and achieve their mission without detection. Tasked mainly with ferrying the Navy's maritime sniper brigades to their objectives in the South during wartime, the fleet was likely produced when the KPAN decided to forgo the strategy of many small (Nampho-class) landing craft in favour of the longer-ranged hovercraft. Since they are faster than most North Korean naval craft, protection of the fleet would mostly occur through scarce air power or whatever torpedo boats could manage to keep up, and its main defensive strategy would therefore be to avoid being spotted at all. On the eastern coast, the entire fleet is located at Unit 291 in Wonsan Bay, slightly over 100 kilometres from the DMZ. On the western coast the fleet is divided between two bases in the far north, with each base chiefly operating either the Kong Bang II or III, but in times of high tension it would likely relocate to new forward operating bases (FOB) near Ryongyong built since early 2010. Another major hovercraft base was seemingly under construction west of Ongjin to facilitate an even faster deployment, but the project was halted in the mid 2010s and subsequently aborted. From Ryongyong hovercraft could make landings on disputed islands near the NLL in under an hour, or quickly assault the South Korean mainland which is under 200 kilometres away. South Korea is acutely aware of the threat posed by the North's hovercraft, and has attempted to mitigate their effectiveness through the introduction of new weaponry dedicated to their destruction. Specifically, the ROKN PKMR-class patrol boat is equipped with an advanced 12-tube 130mm MRL system, which uses guided rockets with a range of over 20 kilometres and an imaging infrared homing seeker to accurately identify their target, which may be a hovercraft or any of the other myriad of small vessels the KPAN employs, in the terminal stage. Additionally, the Republic of Korea Marine Corps fields the Low-Cost Guided Imaging Rocket (LOGIR) as part of the service's Bigung coastal defence system, which is fitted with 2x18 LOGIR 70mm precision-guided rockets. As each of these rockets is capable of disabling or potentially destroying any of the Kong Bang types, any hovercraft force that makes the mistake of coming within its 8km range is sure

The 24-metre hovercraft features circular encasings around its propellers, likely along with other technological advancements. However, it did not enter wide-scale production. (Authors' archive)

to face destruction. If properly deployed during periods of high tensions the PKMR-class and Bigung CDS could provide a potent deterrent to hovercraft attempting to infiltrate Southern waters.

Although the current inventory of hovercraft was mostly built by the mid to late 1990s, the construction of various new bases and the overhaul of old ones on both coasts might indicate that more are to be built in the future. Since the 2000s, investment in new hovercraft technologies have not been at a standstill, with front companies such as the Malaysian Kay Marine Sdn Bhd offering new types of hovercraft for civilian and military use for export, the largest measuring 24 metres in length. These hovercraft feature new design aspects, and most notably have circular encasings for their thrust fans where the examples currently in service do not. This implies advances have been made in their propulsion system, likely increasing top speed and mobility. Other hovercraft that are in service are now often spotted with new Furuno radars, and sometimes carrying two small platforms for MANPADS operators to provide a slim degree of protection from enemy air power.

9

SUBMARINES

As with almost any branch of military technology, North Korea has invested significant resources into acquiring and developing its submarine forces. Although public information on the topic has in the past been scarce, its indigenous ventures in this area were blasted onto headlines across the world when the *Cheonan* was sunk by a North Korean torpedo in March 2010, killing 46 of its crew. Nonetheless, the DPRK's incredibly rich history with submarine warfare dates back well over half a century, which has as such resulted in a diverse adversary with a strong propensity for secrecy – making an accurate assessment of its capabilities a challenge.

With the superiority of the United States' naval forces a given since the Korean War, submarine forces have understandably been a focus point of the KPAN, their defining characteristic negating the vulnerability to enemy vessels and air power inherent to surface combatants. This has over the decades led to a plethora of

highly interesting designs, which include submarines specialised for infiltration purposes, guided-missile submarines and in recent years even ballistic missile submarines (SSBs). Although many of these were destined to remain confined to the drawing boards, the North Korean submarine industry is thriving, with new designs being introduced rapidly and a fledgling strategic capability once more putting the region under the North's nuclear crosshairs. While solid information is scarce, rumours fly wildly and unconfirmed or even certifiably false reports are readily repeated in various analyses. What is known is that almost all of the DPRK's submarines are either of indigenous manufacture or design, the latter of which have been specifically designed with North Korea's unique asymmetrical military tactics in mind. This manifests itself in a clear distinction between hunter-killer submarines and infiltration submarines, often consisting of a single class modified for either use. The attack variants as a rule enter service with the KPAN; the infiltration variants are employed by the Reconnaissance General Bureau.

As with other vessels in the KPAN, North Korea operates a massive number of submarines, competing in numbers with the world powers, yet generally of small size and often bordering on debilitating age. Roughly 70 submarines are in service, of which at least 25 are larger ocean-capable vessels, some 45 smaller coastal submarines and a number of vessels are dedicated to infiltration missions. Similar to other classes of naval ships in the KPAN, the DPRK simply refers to its ship with its purpose and hull number, such as Submarine *No. 748* (for a Type 033-class hunter-killer submarine), or Reconnaissance Submarine *No. 2* (for a Sang O infiltration submarine). Since its submarines are divided amongst a variety of classes and different tasks, some of which explicitly exclude combat confrontations, the North Korean submarine fleet's numerical weight does not directly translate into an offensive threat. Instead, a careful consideration of each craft's capabilities and purposes is required as well as an appreciation of overall North Korean submarine doctrine to assess its true potential. Still, the perceived menace of the DPRK's submarines is certainly one of the KPAN's most feared aspects, as was attested by the concerns raised when much of the submarine fleet left its bases during a period of high tensions in mid 2015. If war does break out, many of its attack submarines will engage enemy combatants along the Korean coasts and attempt to sow confusion in the early stages of mobilisation, while infiltration submarines will be active inserting special forces as part of efforts to create a second front further down the peninsula and possibly in Japan. An addition to its task set comes from the KPAN's newest submarine assets, with the Gorae-class and modified Romeo-class SSBs currently providing the sole operational ocean-based nuclear deterrent available to the DPRK, barring the recent deployment of nuclear-capable weaponry on other submarines. In both peacetime and wartime, intelligence gathering and minelaying provide further niche roles for certain submarines, substantially diversifying the fleet beyond mere offensive operations.

Interest in setting up a submarine branch of its (at the time yet-unfounded) navy was likely piqued very early, with a military pact closed between the Soviet Union and the DPRK in 1949 detailing the delivery of a large array of naval vessels including 30 submarines in exchange for the right to use the North Korean ports of Rajin and Chongjin as staging areas.[1] Although these plans never came to fruition – likely due to the advent of the Korean War – deployment of Soviet submarines in North Korean ports and the construction of a submarine base at Chongjin was reported hence. These deployments must have compounded North Korean interests in the matter, and before the end of the Korean War naval officers were reportedly undergoing submarine training in the Soviet Union.[2] Nonetheless, the actual acquisition of submarines would be delayed after the cessation of hostilities, and the KPAN only began acquiring its first submarines in the 1960s. Two Project 613 Whiskey-class submarines were delivered by the Soviet Union in late 1962 with another two following in the years after, at the time representing a leap in capabilities for the KPAN.[3] However, hands-on experience with submarine warfare was not entirely novel to the DPRK even in these early stages of the Cold War, as experimentation with the production of crude midget submarines to be used for infiltration of the South had already commenced. One such design was found stranded on the banks of the Han River northwest of Seoul on 5 July 1965, apparently after a mission to infiltrate agents into the South had gone awry. Although the incident is notable in that it involved the first indigenous submarine designed by North Korea known to exist, the

The 5.7-metre long infiltration submarine was toured around South Korea after being left stranded by its operators on the banks of the Han river. The craft is now exhibited at the Gyeongnam Unification Hall in Changwon, near Pusan. (KTV)

crudeness of the 5.7-metre long vessel made it rather unremarkable and it is likely the project, which probably entailed the production of a larger number of similar midget submarines, had little influence on the submarines that the DPRK would produce later.

By contrast, the delivery of the four Whiskey-class submarines was much more significant both in the scale of operations, with a length of 76 metres and a 50-plus crew, but also in its offensive capabilities, featuring four bow-facing and two stern-facing 533mm torpedo tubes. Although by the 1960s the Whiskey-class was already superseded by more modern designs of the Soviet Union and United States, the submarines represented the first step towards a navy that is arguably geared towards submarine operations more than that of any other nation in the world. To support these submarines a naval base was erected on Mayang Do, an island on the eastern coast which through numerous expansions has remained the largest submarine base in North Korea, still hosting at least some Whiskey-class submarines in active service despite their staggering age.[4] In the second half of the 1960s, perhaps foreshadowing the additional submarine acquisitions that would occur later, another submarine base was erected near Chaho, also on the eastern coast, featuring underground pens tunnelled into a nearby mountain.

Indeed, during the 1970s another acquisition programme had commenced, entailing the assembly of Type 033 (a copy of the Soviet Project 633 Romeo-class) submarines delivered by China. While some reports speculate four operational Type 033s were first delivered, which are possibly now stationed on the western coast, there is no particular evidence to suggest this is the case, with the first examples being assembled on the eastern coast instead. Although this might have started as early as 1972, most estimates indicate a programme that ran from 1974 to the late 1980s, seeing

At least one Whiskey-class submarine is thought to remain in active service despite its staggering age of over 60 years. (KCBC)

The Project 613 Whiskey-class was North Korea's first large submarine, and made up its entire attack fleet until the 1970s. Constructed in the Soviet Union during the 1950s and based on Second World War-era German Type XXI U-boat technology, four units were delivered to North Korea in the early 1960s. Though not the oldest submarines still in active service worldwide, the Whiskey-class boats in North Korea are certainly the most elusive, with little footage known to exist, and less information still available about their service. While at least one example is believed to continue to serve, another ran aground at Mayang Do's north-eastern end in the mid 2000s and could be seen there until it was salvaged in 2015. The ones that remain likely serve only a training function, and their eight 533mm torpedo tubes, six facing forward and two aft, will probably never be fired in anger. (Artwork by Anderson Subtil)

the construction of some 20 submarines.[5] Despite being nearly as outdated as its older Soviet-delivered ancestors, the Type 033 is still one of the most important North Korean submarine assets, simply due to their large number and the fact that it is one of the few designs in service which is capable of venturing into open seas. At a length of 76.6 metres and a displacement of 1,830 tonnes when submerged, the Type 033 also remains the largest attack submarine in service with the DPRK, yet featuring armament roughly comparable to the older Whiskey-class: six bow-facing and two stern-facing 533mm torpedo tubes. It appears that at least some of the Type 033 submarines have been upgraded with new equipment in the 1990s and after, most likely to improve navigation and communication abilities, but reportedly also upgrading the sonar in the process.[6] Since the late 2010s, some examples have also been observed with a modified, chined segment atop their conning towers, closely matching the configuration on some Chinese Type-035 submarines. The effect of this modification is unknown.

As the sole North Korean submarine type truly capable of venturing out further to sea, the Type 033s will likely see service for decades to come, at least until enough resources have been allocated for their replacement: an unlikely prospect. (KCBC)

Kim Jong Un looks through the periscope of Type 033 submarine *No. 748* during a June 2014 visit to Mayang Do. The LCD screen seen in the top right corner could very well be the most modern piece of equipment onboard the submarine. (KCBC)

The crew of a Type 033 submarine poses for a propaganda shot, the new chined segment atop the conning tower clearly visible. (KCBC)

Acquisition of foreign designs was not entirely limited to the Soviet Union and China however, with one interesting example of Western technology finding its way into North Korea entailing the acquisition of a 14.5-metre long West German civilian research submarine, known as *Sea Horse II*, in 1984. Attempts to import midget submarine technologies from various nations have continued until the present, emphasising the challenges faced with upholding the embargoes barring North Korea from importing military materiel. Still, North Korea appears to have had little problem initiating the development of indigenous designs either, and construction of various classes of small submarines readily began in the 1970s. Various sources on the subject often claimed that this project banked heavily on Yugoslavian technology, either acquired in the form of six 16-metre long submarines imported in the early 1970s or simply as blueprints as early as 1965.[7, 8, 9] However, it is believed Yugoslavia's interests in building midget submarines were raised only in the late 1970s, and no known design matches the purported deliveries to North Korea. Whether the origins of the programme were foreign or not, production picked up in earnest in the 1980s, resulting in some 33 midget submarines of 18 metres length by 1987, not far from the numbers seen today.[10] No images or footage of this elusive early design are publicly available, yet it is presumed to be relatively rudimentary, featuring little armament and a very limited operational range.

Entering production in much smaller numbers in the late 1970s was a design to which the Central Intelligence Agency attributed a length of 21 metres in a 1980s assessment, but which likely concerns the 22-metre long P 4-class submarine, which is itself part of a host of related classes with lengths ranging from close to 19 metres to 29 metres.[11] Constituting the first streamlined indigenous submarine introduced to the KPAN, its small size limits it to coastal operations and infiltration missions, possibly with the aid of a support ship. Much of the information known about the design stems from its export ventures, but also from an embarrassing incident in 1998 where a 22-metre long midget submarine became entangled in fishing nets during an espionage mission off the coast of the South Korean city of Sokcho. While under tow to a South Korean naval base the submarine sank, and when it was salvaged three days later the nine inhabitants were found dead inside, four infiltrators having committed suicide after apparently executing the five crew members of the submarine.

After a six month refurbishment period the submarine entered service with the ROKN for testing and familiarising South Korean ASW personnel with its characteristics. It was retired in the early 2000s, and is now displayed at Chinhae Naval Base. The captured P 4 was remarkable in that its two 533mm torpedo tubes had been welded shut, implying this particular example once served as an attack submarine but was now optimised for infiltration and espionage purposes.[12] For this role it sported a curiously designed double propeller to reduce its noise production at high speeds, a contraption which is absent on later variants. While many features of this class are common to all its subvariants, such as its distinctive conning tower with diver lockout chamber, a retractable snorkel aft and an electrically powered pivotable thruster for faster turning, various modifications to examples examined later are apparent. For instance, a number of about 19-metre long submarines, and possibly one or two around 22 metres in length which were exported to Vietnam in 1996, feature redesigned noses and are outfitted with distinctive yellow distress buoys. This is a reflection of North Korean submarine design: as new technologies and improvements become available, newly produced examples immediately benefit from their introduction, sacrificing homogeneity for individual capabilities. This also means that North Korean submarines were often found to utilise a lot of off-the-shelf equipment; wherever it was possible to import technologies that the DPRK does not produce they were simply acquired from abroad.

The P 4 submarine that was lost in 1998 is lifted onto a quay following its sinking. (ROK MoD)

P 4-class submarines sail surfaced along the Vietnamese coast with their commander in the conning tower. (Comrade Commissar Facebook)

An advanced offshoot of the P 4 design likely entered service in the late 1990s or early 2000s, enlarging the submarine's hull to a length of 29 metres and facilitating a correspondingly larger crew of nine. As a successor to the P 4-class submarine, which is itself only obscurely known in public due to the 1998 Sokcho incident, it evokes less recognition than through the label it was given by foreign intelligence agencies: the Yon O-class.[13] Although as with its predecessors very little information on the type is known from its service in the DPRK, export ventures once again

Another Vietnamese P 4-class submarine. Note the yellow buoy and redesigned bow area, giving it a much more modern appearance compared to the example found in 1998. (Comrade Commissar Facebook)

give a clear image of its capabilities. A 2011 advertising video for the Malaysian-based Kay Marine shipbuilding company showed, amongst a host of other North Korean weaponry, a 29-metre long submarine which was described as the MS 29 – presumably for 'Midget Submarine of 29 metres length'.[14] This description was accompanied by footage of the submarine on dry land at the December 7 Factory in Pyongyang, displaying some of its design features. Interestingly, in the mid 2000s reports of a new class of midget submarine being under development in Iran also emerged, with the first units entering service in 2007. These submarines, named the Ghadir-class in Iran, are close copies of the MS 29, differing mainly in the addition of a sonar pod near the submarine's nose, a storage container in front of the conning tower and some minor hull modifications. Tellingly, an infrared imaging device showcased in the Kay Marine advertisement video is also housed in the conning tower of the Iranian examples alongside the surface search radar, acting as a periscope. Production of this submarine in Iran continued in large numbers at least until 2012, and somewhere between 13 and 21 examples are now in service, making up the mainstay of Iran's submarine forces. Although it is deployed in smaller numbers in North Korea, the MS 29 has attained an infamous status on the peninsula for its involvement in the 2010 *Cheonan* sinking. The submarine involved, described as a Yon O-class by South Korea, broke the ship in two with one of its indigenous 533mm CHT-02D torpedoes (or a close relative to the type), resulting in the deaths of 46 of its crew. Remarkably, some reports indicate that North Korea also attempted to sell the MS 29 to Somali pirates in 2015 at a price of 27 million euros. The same sources claim that the DPRK set up front companies to import German MTU engines to power the vessels.[15] Meanwhile, a model of a 27 metre-long submarine displayed in Myanmar in 2020 displays significant similarities with the P 4 and MS 29 submarines, indicating possible ongoing technological assistance to that country.

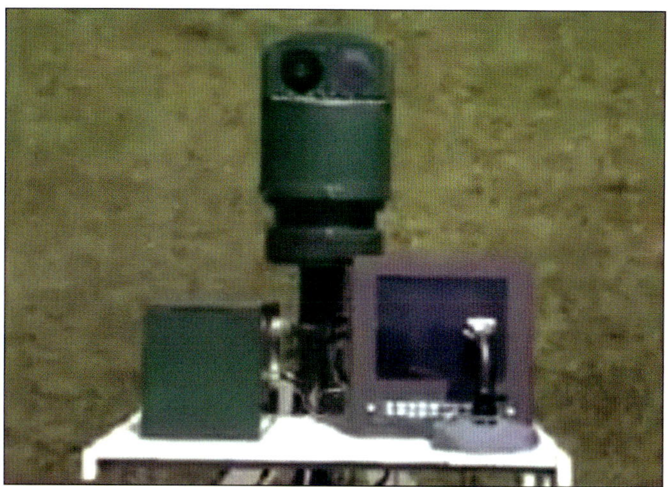

Above: A North Korean MS 29 submarine ashore in Pyongyang. Note that the image's colour pattern has altered through wear, producing an unnaturally blue hue for the submarine. (ROK MoD)

Right: The MS 29's infrared imaging device, also mounted on the examples exported to and produced in Iran. (KCBC)

The rotor section of the torpedo that hit the *Cheonan* on display at the War Memorial of Korea. (ROK MoD)

The *Cheonan* after it had been salvaged following its sinking by a CHT-02D fired from a North Korean submarine. (ROK MoD)

Like its predecessor the P 4-class, the MS 29 (Yon O) is armed with two 533mm torpedo tubes with no reloads. While this limits the potential targets it can engage to a maximum of two, their small size in combination with the powerful 533mm torpedo constitutes a platform perfectly suited to hunter-killer missions along the Korean Peninsula. Furthermore, as these submarines are relatively inexpensive to produce, operate and maintain, their basic design allows the KPAN to produce more submarines and maintain these in a higher level of readiness compared to larger submarines. The potency of this design philosophy was demonstrated in 2010 when a North Korean midget submarine (believed to be a Yon O) managed to remain undetected by the active sonar of the *Cheonan*, later sinking her with a single 533mm torpedo. (Artwork by Anderson Subtil)

A much more ambitious project of the late 1970s, which highlighted an ambition to produce larger submersibles than mere midget submarines, came in the form of a 41-metre long submarine, whose purposes remain largely unclear. Most likely it concerned a single example that turned out not to be successful, and there is reason to believe the prototype sank and was only recovered alongside various other submarines that ran aground on the eastern coast in the early to mid 2010s. A range of other experimental designs such as this one are known, but aside from a 32-metre long submarine (reportedly fitted with external torpedo tubes) built in the early 1980s none appear to have gotten past the drawing board. It is possible that various displayed models and reports of amongst others a 1,000 tonne submarine are related to the same projects however. One of these models, likely originating from the 1990s, depicts in detail a submarine of roughly 40 metres in length, featuring a large sonar dome and four torpedo tubes. This comparatively advanced design incorporates various features from North Korean submarines such as the Whiskey, Type 033 and later indigenous classes. In a bid to establish a salvage and recovery capability to support these designs and other types entering service, the DPRK launched a single 84-metre long submarine rescue ship, designated as the Kowan by the US DoD, on the east coast in the late 1970s. That this ship was incapable of carrying out more advanced rescue operations is attested by the fact that the Soviets undertook a salvage and rescue operation for a North Korean submarine that sank in the East Sea in February 1984.[16]

A project that has had a far more lasting effect on the KPAN's submarine inventory commenced in the 1980s and entailed the construction of a new class of 35-metre long small submarines specialised for various missions. After production picked up in earnest during the early 1990s the type quickly became the most prevalent indigenous submarine design in KPAN service, supplementing the much larger Whiskey and Romeo-class submarines. Famously, one of these submarines optimised for infiltration missions ran aground near the South Korean city of Gangneung in 1996, sparking a 49-day-long manhunt for its surviving crew. The aftermath of this incident included 40 deaths, but also the salvaging and subsequent examination of the submarine, dubbed the Sang O (shark)-class in South Korea, as well as the interrogation of its sole captured crewmember resulting in a wealth of knowledge about North Korea's submarine development programme. Although the attack variant of this submarine was not spotted in video footage until the 2010s, it is believed it was developed alongside the infiltration variant, sporting two or possibly four 533mm torpedoes and no reloads, where in the infiltration variant additional personnel space and a diver lockout chamber is located. Whether both types shares the same propulsion is unknown, although the 3D12 marine diesel

A Romeo-class submarine run aground at Mayang Do. This example was salvaged for scrap years later. (Google Earth – Image © 2019 Digital Globe)

The single Kowan submarine rescue ship constructed for the KPAN. (US DoD)

The interior of the Sang O infiltration submarine. Many of the components were found to be off-the-shelf foreign equipment. (ROK MoD)

This Sang O attack submarine can be discerned from the infiltration variant by the missing protrusion in front of the tower (KCBC)

engine used by the infiltration variant would be very underpowered for an attack submarine. With a displacement of some 370 tonnes when submerged and a crew of 15, the Sang O-class is substantially larger than its predecessors, yet not large enough to exceed the status of a coastal submarine. The large number built on either coast, for a total of over three dozen examples, means the type is likely to be very active during wartime, making up the bulk of the North Korean hunter-killer submarine force alongside the Type 033s. While the Sang O never managed to attract any export orders, it is claimed that

Myanmar had selected the type and was set to order one or two boats before eventually abandoning the idea in 2002.[17] In 2023, following a resumption of arms deals with North Korea amidst the Myanmar civil war, a mystery submarine of approximately 37 metres in length appeared near Rangoon.[18] While its origin remains unknown, technological ties with the Sang O class cannot be ruled out.

During the early 2000s the design was the basis for a variant which increased the total length to some 39 metres, mainly adding hull length aft of the conning tower likely in order to house an upgraded engine, improving over the Sang O's substandard cruising speed and range. Due to a lack of footage other than satellite imagery and the fact that the project represents some of the newest North Korean submarine technology, very little is known about the class, which is sometimes dubbed the 'Sang O II' in foreign media. Improvements may include

The Sang O-class infiltration submarine that ran aground near Gangneung in 1996. (Idobi)

the introduction of two additional torpedo tubes for a total of four, or even experimentation with such technologies as Air-Independent Propulsion (AIP), which allows a submarine a much greater degree of stealth due to a decrease in noise output. Additionally, it may increase the duration for which a submarine can stay submerged by a large factor, generally at the expense of a reduction in power. Although AIP is considered to be highly advanced, North Korea is known not to shy away from attempting to implement modern technologies even when success seems implausible, and the introduction of AIP typically does manifest itself externally in a lengthening of the hull. Such speculation is supported by reports dating to 2019 claiming North Korea had offered Taiwan an indigenous AIP system in 2016, which supposedly allowed a submarine to remain submerged for up to four weeks.[19] Whatever the case, production appears to have included just a handful examples since as early as 2004, almost all of which have been located at Chaho naval base on the eastern coast, with the exception of a single submarine spotted at Pipagot naval base. That the development of small coastal hunter-killer submarines is still very much ongoing is further affirmed by yet another mysterious class of 35-metre long submarines with a distinct teardrop-shaped hull first seen in Nampho in late 2004. Only two have been built, both of which have since remained close to the docks where they were assembled, suggesting they are used as testbeds for new technology or have yet to enter service.

Aside from various small classes of submarines, the DPRK predictably also aspired to produce full-sized attack submarines. Although indigenous designs have indubitably been on the drawing board since the North's submarine programme commenced, the first true indication of larger scale submarine construction concerned reports of a deal to scrap 12 Project 629 'Golf II' and Project 641 'Foxtrot'-class submarines during the 1990s.[20] As these classes are considerably more advanced than the Type 033s that made up the mainstay of its conventional submarine force at the time, it was feared these craft would be refurbished and put back into KPAN service. Whether they actually attempted to do so or even if the deal occurred at all is unclear, but it is certain that no Foxtrot or Golf-II-class submarines entered service, and there is no indication of their associated technologies having any influence on North Korean indigenous designs. No large indigenous submarines managed to find their way into KPAN service throughout the 1990s and 2000s either, but there is some indication that this did not stop North Korean engineers from proposing several designs. One highly interesting, but also extremely elusive, design appears to have concerned an actual guided-missile submarine, presumably fitted with two launchers for the North's advanced P-15/Silkworm missile variants. Aside from the fact that Kim Jong Il was presented with a model of the design in April 1995 nothing is known about its fate, and it appears the plans for its construction simply never came to fruition.

The first stirrings of a far more disturbing development became apparent in the early 2010s, even if at the time it could not be certain what they truly represented. The complete levelling of a village near Sinpho naval base, which was also the site of production of the new 39-metre long submarine at the time, preluded the construction of what turned out to be a ballistic missile testing stand. Completed only in 2014, it soon became clear what the purpose of this testing stand was to be when in August of the same year an entirely novel 67-metre long submarine was suddenly seen berthed in the nearby naval basin. This submarine, initially designated the 'Sinpo'-class by analysts (and the Sinpo-B-class by the US DoD), later became known by its North Korean designation of Gorae (Whale)-class, constituting the first SSB to be built by the DPRK. Being the first completely indigenous submarine design produced for the KPAN in this size class, the fact that it houses a single ballistic missile tube in its conning tower is quite astounding. Furthermore, the same class was utilised not only to experiment with several submarine-launched ballistic missile (SLBM) designs, but in early 2023 even to test the North's first submarine-launched cruise missiles (SLCMs). Given that even amongst economically and technologically advanced nations very few produce SSBs or sub-surface ballistic nuclear submarines (SSBNs), let alone the range of other strategic weapons systems unveiled in the 2010s and 2020s, these feats are undeniably impressive. Even though it is underwhelmingly armed and, for a modern ballistic missile submarine, exceedingly small, seemingly undermining the threat it poses, a few things should be kept in mind when considering its impact on the strategic balance. For one, the Gorae-class is obviously a prototype aimed at testing the feasibility of building an indigenous SSB, and is as such still actively being modified, even to the extent of repeatedly swapping out the type of ballistic missile as new technologies became available. Also, early Russian SSBs, such as the Project 658 Hotel-class, took a similar approach to mounting ballistic missiles on a submarine, indicating North Korea is retracing these developments and is now looking to produce more advanced SSBs. Lastly, even if its capabilities limit it to striking a single target in the direct vicinity of the Korean Peninsula and east Asia, the fact that this capability now exists in the first place is highly significant, substantially expanding upon North Korea's fledgling deterrent.

The Gorae-class submarine surfaces after an October 2021 SLBM test. This was the first test of its new ballistic missile. (KCBC)

The Gorae-class SSB at sunset near Mayang Do. The sail later got the hull number 824, referring to its name of *Hero Ship 8.24* which it received after the first successful SLBM test on the 24 August 2016. (KCBC)

Kim Jong Un inspects the Gorae-class SSB at Mayang Do. (KCBC)

The Gorae is much smaller than any other ballistic missile submarine previously developed anywhere in the world, and consequently only carries one SLBM (in addition to an unknown amount of torpedo tube-launched SLCMs). Owing to its nature as an experimental submarine intended to test emergent SLBM technologies, the Gorae represents the smallest viable platform capable of carrying an SLBM, and likely only possesses a limited operational capability should the need arise. (Artwork by HI Sutton)

Analysis of the Gorae shows the class has a displacement of some 1,650 tonnes submerged and is served by an estimated crew of upwards of 50.[21] At least two torpedo tubes are fitted, but the submarine's experimental nature means that these are likely limited to testing purposes, and may not carry reloads. In March 2023, these were used for the first time as a testbed for a North Korean SLCM, believed to be the Pulhwasal-3. The two missiles launched reportedly had a range of some 1,500 kilometres and are nuclear-capable, thus diversifying the submarine's crude nuclear deterrent. While the Gorae's sonar suite can only be guessed at, the limited nature of its surface search equipment – typically housed in the conning tower, which now shares a ballistic missile launch tube – likewise suggests that the Gorae-class is highly geared towards testing its SLBM and SLCM capabilities only (which will be covered in detail in the final volume in this series).[22] Much of the space aft of the conning tower is likely to be taken up by machinery and engines, presumed to be diesel-electric like other North Korean submarine designs. In summary, the Gorae appears to represent the absolute bare minimum of what constitutes a viable SLBM platform, essentially posing the crudest submarine-based nuclear deterrent possible. Its limited size and accompanying range are matched by its underwhelming armament, similarly lacking in reach to present a credible threat to distant regions, as a more conventional SSBN would. For all its vices, the Gorae-class is characteristic of a profound escalation in the North's nuclear capabilities however, facing off against its neighbours with yet another unexpected and difficult to counter strategic asset. More importantly, it is an ominous prelude

to what is to come, setting the stage for a North Korea with a fully operational sea-based leg of its still fledgling nuclear triad.

While another programme that was to become the pinnacle of its submarine engineering was already underway, North Korea found yet another way to bolster its fledgling sea-based deterrent at relatively low cost. Starting in October 2015, one of its Romeo-class submarines began an extensive overhaul process berthed in one of Sinpho's recently refurbished dry docks. Its real modifications were only fitted after it was brought inside one of Sinpho's new hangars in late 2017 or early 2018 however. In a visit to the facility by Kim Jong Un in July 2019 the full extent of this work became apparent: a hull section nearly eight metres in length was inserted aft of the sail to make room for an SLBM of unknown specification. The resulting submarine measures roughly 84.5-metre long, making it the largest in KPAN service up until that point. Although most of its external features were left unmodified, the sail was modernised and enlarged to make room for the SLBM canister which is fitted to it in the same way as with the Gorae-class, though the missile destined for it may be of a larger type. Mysteriously, the released footage purposely obscured the raised section aft of the sail as well as the sensitive equipment atop the sail, leaving their exact dimensions and specifications unknown. However, it is possible that the characteristic equipment of the Romeo-class's conning tower was left in place slightly sunken in the now higher sail, and the possibility of other new weaponry (such as a smaller SLBM) fitted in the raised aft section cannot be excluded. Many questions about this submarine remain, primarily because as of 2026 it was seemingly still not launched. Given its obvious experimental nature, it may well be that it never attained actual seaworthiness and instead served solely as a testbed of new technologies to come to fruition in future SSBs.

That this may be the case is supported by the fact that in September of 2023 another SSB on the basis of an old Romeo-class submarine was introduced, which though similar in nature features quite a number of substantially different modifications. Given the extent of the differences, it is likely they constitute two different submarines – thus implying a reasonably fast conversion rate even in this experimental phase.[24] The new SSB is referred to as the tactical nuclear attack submarine *No. 841 Hero Kim Gun-Ok*, referencing its offensive weaponry which consists of at least three types of missiles capable of carrying tactical nuclear warheads. Like the older, Romeo-class-

Kim Jong Un inspects the strategic Romeo-based SSB in a facility at Sinpho in 2019. The sail with its missile tube is clearly visible, although the section aft of it has been pixelated. (KCBC)

based SSB, it has had a segment added aft of its sail, adding almost 10 metres in length to the submarine to make it the largest currently in service. The sail itself has been similarly streamlined as well, though it is smaller due to omission of the integrated SLBM launch tube, and features diving planes as well as a chined segment housing the submarine's periscope, surface search radar and antennas. Aft of the sail, a massive raised platform houses the *Hero Kim Gun-Ok*'s main offensive armament: four tubes thought to contain small SLBMs like the Hwasong-11S, and another six believed to contain SLCMs like the Pulhwasal-3. While the propulsion of the Romeo-class appears unchanged, the bow of the boat was significantly altered; conspicuously rounded and seemingly lacking even the Romeo's very modest sonar array, it features six torpedo tubes arranged two at a side. These presumably too can be used to launch SLCMs, bringing the total complement to four SLBMs and 12 SLCMs, assuming no reloads. A crew complement of 50 was observed during its launching ceremony at Sinpho, and many of the main internal components of the submarine are likely to be different from the Romeo-class. Nevertheless, the fact that it is substantially less hydrodynamically optimised and apparently has an unaltered propulsion system means it probably suffers from even more severe noise and mobility-related detractions than that 1950s design.

Although these new Romeo modifications obviously inherit the same vices of their age-old Soviet ancestor and are limited in their use in a similar way to the purpose-built Gorae-class SSB, their construction opens up a world of possibilities for the KPAN given the large number of platforms available for conversion, and comparatively impressive construction speed. Should the new SSBs prove to be successful in their role, they will also provide additional problems for opposing forces which are then faced with tracking and destroying every Romeo-class submarine on the east coast to prevent the SSBs among them from striking their target. While these submarines will likely be unable to venture out to sea far enough to allow a strike on the US mainland, the North's press statements attest that their operational area will cover the East Sea, thus setting the entirety of Korea and Japan in their sights.

Beyond its SSB programme, which currently appears to be the primary focus of the DPRK's submarine development efforts, it is unknown what the future will hold for conventional North Korean submarine technology. Although its first ventures into building large submarines might seem like an opportunity to explore larger classes of attack submarines as well, it should be realised that the KPAN still maintains only a limited production capability. As such, investment in new full-sized submarines might be deemed unsound, and further development of small attack submarines such as the new 39-metre long class favoured instead. The introduction of new weaponry, including more advanced torpedoes and submarine-launched cruise missiles, may therefore be a more attractive research objective.

Beyond the conventional however, there is ample indication where North Korea's ambitions lie. During the 8th Congress of the WPK in 2021, one of the key technologies that Kim Jong Un declared as part of the North's intentions was a nuclear-powered submarine, confirming that the DPRK had indeed set its sights on this most ambitious of submarine technologies.[25] Intriguingly, there are some indications that this has been a much longer standing goal however, with a tentative project believed to exist as early as 2009 aiming for the construction of an SSB by 2015, and a nuclear-powered submarine by 2020. While the former was technically achieved, the first indications of work on a successor class for the Gorae SSB (dubbed the 'Sinpo-C' by the US DoD), at the renovated construction site at Sinpho naval base (known as the Pongdae submarine factory), only came five years prior to the deadline set. The open-air parts storage site at that facility, aside from indicating that assembly was already underway in late 2015, offered up details of a range of components waiting to be installed, including hull cross sections measuring roughly 11 metres in diameter. This diameter far exceeds that of the Gorae-class, let alone any other North Korean submarine yet produced, and is consistent with a more traditional form factor for SSB(N)s. The design might well have benefitted from technology obtained from the major South Korean shipbuilder Daewoo Shipbuilding & Marine Engineering, which was hacked by North Korean cyberwarfare operatives in April 2016. About 60 classified military documents with information and possibly blueprints of ROKN warships, submarines and 'cold launch' technology were among the some 40,000 documents retrieved.

The start of assembly evidently did not prevent ongoing design adjustments however. While the submarine remained hidden from

At some 85 metres in length, the *Hero Kim Gun-Ok* is the largest submarine operated by the KPAN. Echoes of its Romeo-class roots are evident, and the incorporation of a streamlined sail creates a peculiar fusion of antiquity and modernity. (KCBC)

A view of the hump housing the missile compartment on the *Hero Kim Gun-Ok*. Out of the 10 vertical launch tubes, four are dedicated for launching submarine-launched ballistic missiles while the remaining six are intended for launching cruise missiles. (KCBC)

The new strategic SSB based on a modified Romeo-class. A roughly eight metre long section was added directly aft of the much modernised and enlarged sail, behind which a raised section with an as of yet unknown purpose was fitted. Note that the propeller, torpedo tubes and sonar were left unmodified. As this artwork is based on currently available imagery, the final configuration might differ from what can be seen here. (Artwork by Anderson Subtil)

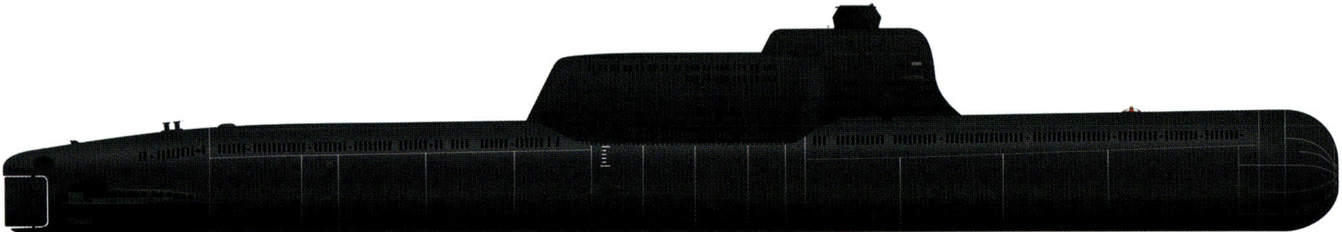

The new tactical SSB *Hero Kim Gun-Ok* based on a modified Romeo-class. Like the earlier Romeo-based SSB, it features extensive modifications and had a segment inserted to facilitate the fitting of SLBMs and SLCMs. Although the propeller section was blurred in state media, it appears unchanged from the original Romeo-class. (Artwork by Anderson Subtil)

the public eye, a series of ever larger new SLBMs spawned by its ballistic missile programme suggested shifting specifications. No less than four different SLBMs at one time or another were thought to be destined for the new submarine, with the majority still lacking a launch platform. Kim Jong Un's remarks in 2021 were the first sign that the project was nearing completion, claiming that the design had at last been finalised. In early 2024, another state media report affirmed that the project was still underway, though there was no indication of how far it had progressed. By October however, South Korea's Defense Intelligence Agency suggested construction on a largest-yet, possibly nuclear-powered submarine had commenced. Telling of the DPRK's ambitions with regard to their newly founded SSB programme, a large new dock and pier to accommodate their future SSB force are simultaneously under construction at a slow pace, possibly matching the launch date of the 'Sinpo-C'. Further expansions of historically commercial docks in Sinpho might be similarly linked to this new project, as such constituting some of the largest new submarine bases under development since the previous century.

The first concrete indications that the SSBN project was finally bearing fruit came in March 2025, when state media covered visits to major shipbuilding industries by Kim Jong Un. While the footage and accompanying commentary disclosed little of substance about the largest North Korean submarine programme yet, it referred to the vessel as a 'nuclear-powered strategic guided missile-launching submarine', affirming its nuclear propulsion system while maintaining a degree of ambiguity about its armament. Interestingly, the estimated diameter of the submarine displayed was a good match for the hull components of the Sinpo-C spotted in the mid-2010s, suggesting both projects are indeed one and the same. While it is possible that Russian financing, imported components and technical assistance are helping to finalise the project now, testimony given during the 8th Congress of the WPK in 2021 claiming that 'the design of a new nuclear submarine is complete and in the final review stage' suggests that major design elements like its nuclear

reactor predate the countries' recent rapprochement and arms deals. Moreover, given that North Korean experience operating and designing reactors (including a small experimental light water reactor at Nyongbyon) now dates back over half a century, submarine-compatible reactor technology should be within reach. The extremely protracted development, from initial plans in 2009 through beginning of construction in 2015, design consolidation in 2020 and a possible launch date in 2026, means the programme likely faced multiple hurdles and course corrections. Given the diverse design constraints on submarine nuclear reactors, including small size, appropriate shielding and cooling systems, high fuel economy and silent operation, it's likely that the reactor has been the primary obstacle. Since no radiation signature or cooling water dumping has yet been detected, it does not appear the reactor is operational, casting doubt on the actual introduction date of the submarine. Should the DPRK succeed in developing this powerful technology however, it will offer the country a leap in abilities over anything previously available, including improved speed, endurance, noise reduction and ability to stay submerged.

In December 2025, Kim Jong Un once more visited the Pongdae submarine factory, with state media coverage unveiling the SSBN had been largely completed. The design showcased reportedly displaces 8,700 tonnes (submerged, presumably), and is estimated to be approximately 105 metres in length. Despite its, by North Korean standards, very large size, serious design compromises are apparent to accommodate the up to 14-metre-long SLBMs intended for this submarine. Rather than featuring a dedicated raised segment housing the missile compartment, as has become the standard on most modern SSB(N)s, the missiles tubes remain integrated in the sail, which is elongated to some 35 metres in total. As many as 10 SLBMs are believed to be fitted, arranged in a single row with launch tube hatches alternately opening to either side. The sail and prominent raised deck running along the length of the submarine likely have a detrimental effect on its noise levels and aquadynamics, with the added risk of making the vessel top-heavy.

Kim Jong Un inspects the DPRK's first nuclear-powered submarine at Sinpho in early 2025. Note that two different photos were merged to establish the appearance of a larger submarine. (KCBC)

This weight is offset somewhat by two very large (approximately 40-metre-long) conformal sonar arrays, forming a ridge along the submarine's lower sides. Six torpedo tubes in the bow leave ample room for another bow-mounted sonar array, although the specifications of either array can only be guessed at. Although the stern (and screw) are not visible in available imagery, stern-facing torpedo tubes were likely omitted.

Much of the submarine's intended operational role is dependent on the capabilities of its (as yet untested) SLBMs. Being of comparable size and configuration to foreign long-ranged SLBMs like the UGM-133 Trident II and JL-2, its maximum range will determine whether regular long-distance deployments to the Pacific Ocean are required to maintain a credible deterrent, or if (parts of) mainland USA are within reach from the East Sea. In the latter case, stealth, operational range, and speed may not be a primary design consideration. Instead, its operational area may remain confined to relatively close-by waters, obviating the need to pass well-patrolled chokepoints around Japan and South Korea. Whatever the case, it is clear the submarine is intended for operational use, such that the KPAN is now moving towards a more practical, rather than rudimentary or demonstrative, sea-based leg of its nuclear deterrent. Whether that will be a success remains to be seen, and many hurdles remain in the way of its operational deployment.

While the DPRK has invested heavily in exploiting any opportunity to introduce new technologies into its navy since the 1990s, this has yet to translate into a significant increase in the actual wartime capabilities of its surface fleet. While its immense fleet of vessels of different types allows the KPAN to maintain its status as an intimidating coastal navy power, its surface vessels would find themselves at odds with at least two greatly superior navies. A lack of offensive means to effectively target enemy combatants further out to sea and a lack of defensive means against enemy aircraft could prevent many KPAN ships from ever sighting their enemy, let alone moving into firing range. Furthermore, actual preparedness levels within the KPAN appear to be quite low and should a war break out many of its combatants could be caught stored on land or without munitions. In an age where the ROKN and USN enjoy a massive technological advantage in conventional warfare, the DPRK's best bet at maintaining what inventory and deterrence it has today ironically lies with the fast attack craft it previously rejected for its own navy. Capable of being armed with AShMs and easily mass-produced at low cost within a short time frame, large numbers of such missile-armed FACs operated in conjunction with sizeable numbers of small submarines and coastal defence missile systems could ensure the KPAN maintains a viable combat capacity. For the DPRK, these represent the most cost-effective method of maintaining a force capable of projecting power around the Korean Peninsula, further exploiting this area of asymmetrical warfare as they have done successfully for the past decades. Be that as it may, the KPAN seems unwilling to content itself with a role in securing the DPRK's coastal waters. Instead, its maritime planners have apparently envisioned a bold offensive doctrine for its future naval forces that includes both 'blue water' capabilities and a central role in the country's strategic deterrence. The maxim 'go big or go home' has become a core tenet on the seas and in the other military branches; whether that was a wise decision only time will tell.

The new SSBN at the Pongdae submarine factory in December 2025. Note the red anti-fouling paint; a darker top-coating has presumably yet to be applied to the upper half. (KCBC)

A closeup of the sail of the new SSBN, showcasing its large diving planes and mixed set of optronic masts (and/or periscopes). (KCBC)

BIBLIOGRAPHY

Bermudez Jr., Joseph S. *Shield of the Great Leader: The Armed Forces of North Korea* (St Leonards: Allen & Unwin, 2001)

Federal Research Division. *North Korea a country study* (Washington, DC.: Federal Research Division, 2008)

James Martin Center for Nonproliferation Studies at the Monterey Institute of International Studies *North Korea Missile Chronology* (Washington, DC.: Nuclear Threat Initiative, 2012)

Kim Il-Sung. *The present situation and the tasks of our party; report at the conference of the Workers' Party of Korea* (Pyongyang: Foreign Languages Pub, 1966)

Marine Corps Intelligence Activity. *North Korea Country Handbook* (Quantico: Marine Corps Intelligence Activity, 1997)

Ministry of National Defence of the Republic of Korea. *Defense White Papers 2006-2018* (Yongsan, Seoul: Ministry of National Defence of the Republic of Korea, 2006-2018)

Tertitskiy, F. The North Korean Army: *History, Structure, Daily Life (1st ed.)* (Routledge, 2022)

ENDNOTES

Introduction

1 We forsook the opportunity to use KPAAAAF.

2 Artworks in this book series serve mainly to elucidate subjects of which appropriate imagery is lacking, and as such certain volumes contain noticeably larger numbers of artworks than others.

3 Ambassador Han Duck-soo. 'Briefing -the Cheonan Situation' (2010) *Center for Strategic and International Studies* https://csis-prod.s3.amazonaws.com/s3fs-public/legacy_files/files/attachments/100525_AMB_Briefing-2.pdf

Chapter 1

1 Ed Evanhoe. 'US Navy Ships: Sunk or Damaged in Action during the Korean Conflict' *Naval History and Heritage Command* http://www.korean-war.com/USNavy/usnavyshipssunk.html

2 DPR Korea. 'Outstanding Leadership and Brilliant Victory' (1993) *Wilson Center* https://digitalarchive.wilsoncenter.org/document/155225

3 HI Sutton. 'Captured UUV in Pyongyang North-Korea' (2020) *Cover Shores* http://www.hisutton.com/Captured-UUV-in-Pyongyang-North-Korea.html

4 HI Sutton. 'Captured UUV in Pyongyang North-Korea' (2020) *Cover Shores* http://www.hisutton.com/Captured-UUV-in-Pyongyang-North-Korea.html

5 North Korea claims the exact opposite: that South Korean warships had entered North Korean territorial waters.

6 Korean Central News Agency. 'Statement today over the armed conflict that took place' (1999) *KCNA* http://www.kcna.co.jp/item/1999/9906/news06/19.htm

7 The Dong-a Ilbo. '13 NK Seamen Killed in 2002 Inter-Korean Naval Battle' (2009) *Donga* https://www.donga.com/en/article/all/20090629/262546/1

Chapter 2

1 Chad O'Carroll. 'At least 24 N. Korean sailors dead in E. Coast naval accident' (2013) *NK News* https://www.nknews.org/2013/11/at-least-24-n-korean-sailors-dead-in-e-coast-naval-accident/

2 KCNA. 'Respected Comrade Kim Jong Un's Speech at Ceremony of Launching Destroyer of Navy of Korean People's Army' (2025) *KCNA Watch* https://kcnawatch.org/newstream/1745803013-145914096/respected-comrade-kim-jong-uns-speech-at-ceremony-of-launching-destroyer-of-navy-of-korean-peoples-army/

Chapter 3

1 Central Intelligence Agency. 'Naval Base Wonsan Munchon, North Korea' (1966) *CIA FOIA* https://www.cia.gov/readingroom/document/cia-rdp78t05929a002200090008-0

2 Nuclear Threat Initiative. 'North Korean Missile Chronology' (2012) *Nuclear Threat Initiative* https://www.nti.org/media/pdfs/north_korea_missile_2.pdf?_=1327534760?_=1327534760

3 The Korean word for Venus; North Korean missile classes are typically named after celestial bodies.

4 Central Intelligence Agency. 'Naval Base Wonsan Munchon, North Korea' *CIA FOIA* https://www.cia.gov/readingroom/document/cia-rdp79-00849a001200010008-2

5 Daniel Salisbury. 'How North Korea built an expansive military hovercraft force from UK designs' (2025) *NK News* https://www.nknews.org/2025/02/how-north-korea-built-an-expansive-military-hovercraft-force-from-uk-designs/

6 Central Intelligence Agency. 'Construction And Modification Of North Korean Naval Combatants, January 1983 Through July 1986' (1987) *CIA FOIA* https://www.cia.gov/readingroom/document/cia-rdp87t00758r000103060001-8

7 Central Intelligence Agency. 'Communist Military Assistance to Nicaragua: Trends and Implications' (1987) *CIA FOIA* https://www.cia.gov/readingroom/document/cia-rdp97r00694r000800340001-5

8 SAR Staff. 'Weapons of the Nicaraguan Army Naval Force' (1987) *Small Arms Review* https://smallarmsreview.com/weapons-of-the-nicaraguan-army-naval-force/

9 Central Intelligence Agency. North Korean Activities Overseas' (1984) *CIA FOIA* https://www.cia.gov/readingroom/document/cia-rdp85t00310r000200050003-7

10 Central Intelligence Agency. 'Construction And Modification Of North Korean Naval Combatants, January 1983 Through July 1986' (1987) *CIA FOIA* https://www.cia.gov/readingroom/document/cia-rdp87t00758r000103060001-8

11 Central Intelligence Agency. 'Construction And Modification Of North Korean Naval Combatants, January 1983 Through July 1986' (1987) *CIA FOIA* https://www.cia.gov/readingroom/document/cia-rdp87t00758r000103060001-8

12 Central Intelligence Agency. 'MISSILE-EQUIPPED COMBATANTS TOEJO-DONG NAVAL BASE AND MISSILE SUPPORT FACILITY, NORTH KOREA (SANITIZED)' (1982) CIA FOIA https://www.cia.gov/readingroom/document/cia-rdp90t00784r000100110012-0

13 Central Intelligence Agency. 'Construction And Modification Of North Korean Naval Combatants, January 1983 Through July 1986'

Chapter 4

1 Central Intelligence Agency. 'SIGNIFICANCE AND IMPLICATIONS OF THE NORTH KOREAN-LIBYAN FRIENDSHIP TREATY' (1982) *CIA FOIA* https://www.cia.gov/readingroom/document/cia-rdp85t00153r000100040017-9

2 Joseph S. Bermudez Jr., *Shield of the Great Leader: The Armed Forces of North Korea* (St Leonards NSW: Allen & Unwin, 2001)

3   Nuclear Threat Initiative. 'North Korean Missile Chronology' (2012) *Nuclear Threat Initiative* https://www.nti.org/media/pdfs/north_korea_missile_2.pdf?_=1327534760?_=1327534760

4   Such as its extremely low 'sea-skimming' flight altitude and employment of an active radar which can reportedly detect its own targets at a range of 20 kilometres, and be detected only at roughly seven, which, with a speed of Mach 0.8, leaves less than a minute response time.

5   These reports are occasionally also tied to a supposed land-attack cruise missile variant. Although North Korea has implied the existence of such missiles in propaganda material, there is as yet no conclusive evidence to corroborate this.

6   Central Intelligence Agency 'Iraq WMD 2004 – Delivery Systems' (2004) *CIA* https://www.cia.gov/library/reports/general-reports-1/iraq_wmd_2004/chap3.html

7   Pulhwasal means 'Fire Arrow'; it is unclear what earns it this name instead of just Hwasal, and whether or not a Pulhwasal-1 and 2 exist.

Chapter 5

1   An alternative possibility that these two stations can be fitted with two MANPADS each to serve as a rudimentary air-defence capability cannot be excluded.

2   Practically all heavier weaponry on modern KPAN craft have the option of being operated manually, perhaps because North Korea expects heavy jamming of their guidance systems and hopes to retain some of their use under such circumstances.

3   While the use of these radars might seem unorthodox, almost all vessels in the KPAN actually use a variety of Furuno and (scarce) Koden radars since the 1960s acquired via the civilian market, and certain types are in use with a range of foreign military naval vessels as well.

4   In this configuration the SSES III bears a remarkable similarity in its armament, general capabilities and combat role to the Republic of China Navy's Tuo Jiang-class, which is often billed by the media as a 'carrier killer'. Of course, aircraft carriers are notoriously difficult to destroy, and SSES III appears to be geared more towards stealthy hunter-killer missions along the Korean coasts.

5   Tarao '断念？それとも完成？10年以上も造船所┌に放置された北朝鮮の新型ミサイル艇の動' (2022) *Deep Dive* https://note.com/tarao727/n/nd2d1dc728d75

Chapter 6

1   Information obtained from a report by the Burmese Military High-Level Representatives, led by the Member of the State Peace and Development Council and Chief of Coordination (Army, Navy, Air Force) General Thura Shwe Mann, that went on an observation trip to the Democratic People's Republic of Korea and People's Republic of China from (21) November 2008 to (2) December 2008.

2   Named for the Tuman River, which forms part of the border between North Korea and its neighbours, China and Russia.

3   After the Amnok River that makes up a major portion of the border separating North Korea and China.

4   KCNA. 'Respected Comrade Kim Jong Un Oversees Performance Test of Drones' (2024) *KCNA Watch* https://kcnawatch.org/newstream/1724624022-838255186/respected-comrade-kim-jong-un-oversees-performance-test-of-drones/

5   Ryo Hinata-Yamaguchi. 'North Korea faces daunting challenge in modernizing its archaic naval fleet' (2023) *NK News* https://www.nknews.org/pro/north-korea-faces-daunting-challenge-in-modernizing-its-archaic-naval-fleet/

6   Korean Central News Agency. 'Respected Comrade Kim Jong Un Gives Field Guidance to Nampho Dockyard' (2024) *KCNA Watch* https://kcnawatch.org/newstream/1706827068-648651747/respected-comrade-kim-jong-un-gives-field-guidance-to-nampho-dockyard/

7   Minju Choson. 'Respected Comrade Kim Jong Un Inspects Site for Construction of New Naval Base' (2024) *KCNA Watch* https://kcnawatch.org/newstream/1725800537-837933847/respected-comrade-kim-jong-un-inspects-site-for-construction-of-new-naval-base/

8   Peter Makowsky, Jack Liu, Martyn Williams and Iliana Ragnone. 'Major Construction at Nampho Port' (2024) *38 North* https://www.38north.org/2024/09/major-construction-at-nampho-port/

9   Colin Zwirko. 'North Korea preparing to move large new warship in sign of advanced development' (2025) *NK News* https://www.nknews.org/pro/north-korea-preparing-to-move-large-new-warship-in-sign-of-advanced-development/

10   After the anti-Japanese revolutionary Choe Hyon (1907-1982).

11   An alternative possibility is that the larger Hwasal variant is compatible with the (larger) Pyoljji-1 VLS cells, which would help explain the decision to introduce a smaller class of cruise missiles to fit the smaller VLS cells.

12   GreatPoppo. '北朝鮮の新型多目的┌逐艦を考察する' (2025) Deep Dive https://note.com/tarao727/n/n3a90ad883f4f

13   KCNA. 'Respected Comrade Kim Jong Un Makes Speech at Ceremony of Launching Destroyer of Navy of Korean People's Army' (2025) KCNA Watch https://kcnawatch.xyz/newstream/1750035855-49634432/respected-comrade-kim-jong-un-makes-speech-at-ceremony-of-launching-destroyer-of-navy-of-korean-peoples-army/

14   GreatPoppo. '北朝鮮の新型多目的┌逐艦を考察する' (2025) Deep Dive https://note.com/tarao727/n/n3a90ad883f4f

15   KCNA. 'Respected Comrade Kim Jong Un Makes Speech at Ceremony of Launching Destroyer of Navy of Korean People's Army' (2025) KCNA Watch https://kcnawatch.xyz/newstream/1750035855-49634432/respected-comrade-kim-jong-un-makes-speech-at-ceremony-of-launching-destroyer-of-navy-of-korean-peoples-army/

16   nK Insight. 'The First New Destroyer 'CHOI HYUN' update #1 : Engine installation at last — Sep 17, 2025' (2025) *SI Analytics* https://si-analytics.ai/the-first-new-destroyer-choi-hyun-update-1-engine-installation-at-last-%e2%80%95-sep-17-2025/

17   nK Insight. 'Additional construction of New Naval Combatant at Chongjin Shipyard — February 18, 2025' (2025) *SI Analytics* https://si-analytics.ai/additional-construction-of-new-naval-combatant-at-chongjin-shipyard-%E2%80%95-february-18-2025/

18   Wisps of smoke swelling up from its exhaust did however suggest at least some of its propulsion and/or power systems were installed.

19   Colin Zwirko. 'North Korea preparing to move large new warship in sign of advanced development' (2025) *NK News* https://www.nknews.org/pro/north-korea-preparing-to-move-large-new-warship-in-sign-of-advanced-development/

20   Pyongyang Times. 'Respected Comrade Kim Jong Un visits destroyer Choe Hyon and learns about training and life of sailors' (2025) *KCNA Watch* https://kcnawatch.org/newstream/1755767436-812556671/respected-comrade-kim-jong-un-visits-destroyer-choe-hyon-and-learns-about-training-and-life-of-sailors/

21   KCNA. 'Respected Comrade Kim Jong Un Visits Destroyer Choe Hyon according to 2nd Day Schedule of Visit related to Military Hardware Exhibition' (2025) *KCNA Watch* https://kcnawatch.org/newstream/1759803445-61239257/respected-comrade-kim-jong-un-visits-destroyer-choe-hyon-according-to-2nd-day-schedule-of-visit-related-to-military-hardware-exhibition/

22   KCNA. 'Respected Comrade Kim Jong Un's Speech at Ceremony of Launching Destroyer of Navy of Korean People's Army' (2025) *KCNA Watch* https://kcnawatch.org/newstream/1745803013-145914096/respected-comrade-kim-jong-uns-speech-at-ceremony-of-launching-destroyer-of-navy-of-korean-peoples-army/

23   KCNA. 'Respected Comrade Kim Jong Un Makes Speech at Ceremony of Launching Destroyer of Navy of Korean People's Army' (2025) *KCNA Watch* https://kcnawatch.xyz/newstream/1750035855-49634432/respected-comrade-kim-jong-un-makes-speech-at-ceremony-of-launching-destroyer-of-navy-of-korean-peoples-army/

24   Iliana Ragnone and Peter Makowsky. 'Quick Take: Chongjin Destroyer Recovery Efforts Continue' *38 North* https://www.38north.org/2025/05/quick-take-chongjin-destroyer-recovery-efforts-continue/

25   Voice of Korea. 'Nampho Shipyard resolved to build "Choe Hyon"-class destroyer No. 3 until founding anniversary of WPK next year' (2025) *KCNA Watch* https://kcnawatch.org/newstream/1753175025-237541191/nampho-shipyard-resolved-to-build-choe-hyon-class-destroyer-no-3-until-founding-anniversary-of-wpk-next-year/

Chapter 7

1   In fact, the warhead of a regular 533mm Type 65 torpedo is roughly twice as heavy as the entire 324mm torpedo.
2   Global Communications Co 'GS-2600-01 UAV/USV Video, Telemetry/Control System' *Glocom* https://glocom-corp.com/2018/index.php/product/detail?p=gs-2600-01
3   Mun Dong Hui. 'Kim Jong Un orders mass production of high-speed torpedo boats' (2018) *Daily NK* https://www.dailynk.com/english/kim-jong-un-orders-mass-production-of-high-speed-torpedo-boats/

Chapter 8

1   Daniel Salisbury. 'How North Korea built an expansive military hovercraft force from UK designs' (2025) *NK News* https://www.nknews.org/2025/02/how-north-korea-built-an-expansive-military-hovercraft-force-from-uk-designs/

Chapter 9

1   Central Intelligence Agency 'Soviet Naval Activity in North Korea' (1949) *CIA FOIA* https://www.cia.gov/readingroom/document/cia-rdp82-00457r003800320004-5
2   Central Intelligence Agency. 'Soviet Submarine Training For North Korean Naval Officers' (1953) *CIA FOIA* https://www.cia.gov/readingroom/document/cia-rdp80-00810A001100870004-0
3   Central Intelligence Agency. 'Preliminary Report, North Korea, No 1' (1962) *CIA FOIA* https://www.cia.gov/readingroom/document/cia-rdp89b00569r000900140038-0
4   Central Intelligence Agency. 'USSR-North Korea: Prospects For Military Cooperation' (1985) *CIA FOIA* https://www.cia.gov/readingroom/document/cia-rdp85t01058r000507530001-6
5   Although some claim it ended only in 1996.
6   Marine Corps Intelligence Activity. 'North Korea Country Handbook' (1997) *Federation Of American Scientists* https://fas.org/nuke/guide/dprk/nkor.pdf
7   HI Sutton. 'North Korean Submarines' (2017) *COVERT SHORES* http://www.hisutton.com/North_Korean_Submarines.html
8   Covert Shores Naval Warfare Blog. 'North Korean Small Submarines File' (2010) http://covertshores.blogspot.com/2010/06/north-korean-small-submarines-file.html
9   Joseph S. Bermudez Jr. 'The North Korean Navy Acquires a New Submarine' (2014) *38 North* https://www.38north.org/2014/10/jbermudez101914/

10   Due to aforementioned confusing circumstances regarding the origin of this technology, these are often referred to as the Yugo-class. This has been the cause of much unclarity, and there is no reason to believe this designation is reflective of any aspect of reality.
11   Central Intelligence Agency. 'Construction and Modification of North Korean Naval Combatants, January 1983 through July 1986' (1987) *CIA FOIA* https://www.cia.gov/readingroom/document/cia-rdp87t00758r000103060001-8
12   It is sometimes reported earlier production examples used 450mm torpedoes.
13   Also stylised as Yono, Yeono or Yeoneo, meaning 'Salmon' in Korean. Although it is uncertain whether this is its actual designation in the DPRK, the use of aquatic species as class designations does match with North Korean practice.
14   Information obtained from Kay Marine Sdn Bhd.
15   Jeon Kyung-woong. '北, 소말리아 해적에 '연어급 잠수정' 팔려다 실패' (2018) https://www.newdaily.co.kr/site/data/html/2018/07/19/2018071900078.html
16   Central Intelligence Agency. 'USSR-North Korea: Prospects For Military Cooperation' (1985) *CIA FOIA* https://www.cia.gov/readingroom/document/cia-rdp85t01058r000507530001-6
17   Andrew Selth. 'Is Burma really buying submarines?' (2014) *Lowy Institute* https://www.lowyinstitute.org/the-interpreter/burma-really-buying-submarines
18   H I Sutton. 'Myanmar's Mystery Submarine' (2024) *Covert Shores* http://www.hisutton.com/Myanmar-Submarine-2023.html
19   Sophia Yang. 'North Korea pitched state-of-the-art submarine system to Taiwan military: report' (2019) *Taiwan News* https://www.taiwannews.com.tw/en/news/3673918
20   Joseph S. Bermudez Jr. 'North Korea: Test Stand for Vertical Launch of Sea-Based Ballistic Missiles Spotted' (2014) *38 North* https://www.38north.org/2014/10/jbermudez102814/
21   HI Sutton. 'Analysis – Sinpo Class Ballistic Missile Sub' (2016) *Covert Shores* http://www.hisutton.com/Analysis%20-%20Sinpo%20Class%20Ballistic%20Missile%20Sub.html
22   The only visible equipment seems to be a searchlight, but other small retractable surface search radars and periscopes are likely.
23   United Nations Security Council. 'Report of the Panel of Experts established pursuant to resolution 1874 (2009)' 5 March 2018.
24   A fact further underlined by indications that a new submarine possibly of the same type is already under construction.
25   Ruediger Frank. 'Key Results of The Eighth Party Congress in North Korea (Part 2 of 2)' (2021) *38 North* https://www.38north.org/2021/01/key-results-of-the-eighth-party-congress-in-north-korea-part-2-of-2/

ABOUT THE AUTHORS

Joost Oliemans is an analyst and author focusing on Asia, the Middle East and North Africa. Together with Stijn Mitzer, he is the author of *The Armed Forces of North Korea: On the Path of Songun*. Joost Oliemans also writes for various news agencies and websites about military-related matters.